WHO MAKES THE BED?

7 Steps into Nurturing Intimacy Beyond the Myth

VIOLA EDWARD

Copyright ©Viola Edward
Date first Published: 23 January 2017, London
ISBN-13: 978-1542415507

All rights reserved

No part of this book may be reproduced in any form, by photocopying or by any electronic or mechanical means, including information storage or retrieval systems, Without permission in writing from both the copyright owner and the publisher of this book.

To my husband, Michael de Glanville, my lover and my friend, the one who can create and express intimacy with words, as well.

All the poems included in this book are his.

About the Book

Loving relationships in our lives go through many different stages over the years and Intimacy between the partners is an essential quality every step of the way. This book is filled with a treasure of clarifying insights and detailed knowledge about the contribution of Intimacy to successful relationship. Learn to create and nurture the development of Intimacy as a vital aspect of friendship between the partners, as well as a lively and flourishing source of the joys and pleasures of their sexuality beyond the associated myths of youth, physical wellness and culture.

I am using my and Michael's story as the central theme for this book, but all of the thoughts and suggestions, which flow from it have been augmented over the years I have worked with couples - straight and same sex - as a psychotherapist and coach.

Contents

About the Book iv

My Story About: Who Makes the Bed? vii

Acknowledgments ix

Foreword xi

Chapter One: Falling in and Out of Love 1

   Love's Song 6

Chapter Two: Love and Intimacy 7

   Owning what has always been mine 11

Chapter Three: The Flow of Communication 13

   Between two souls. 21

Chapter Four: Paradigms and Limiting Thought Habits: 'The Personal Law' 23

Chapter Five: The Transformation of Sexuality 63

   Wide Horizons 68

Chapter Six: Daring to be Sexually Healthy 69

   The Colour of my love. 74

Chapter Seven: The Healing Process of Shared Vision 75

   Crossing the Ocean. 119

Chapter Eight: The Couple as Successful Business Partners 121

   Wind kissed waves. 130

Chapter Nine: Healing Addiction Revives Intimacy 131

Desolation...*139*

Chapter Ten: The Rhythm of the Breath **141**

About this journey of life...*151*

Chapter Eleven: Image and Intimacy **153**

Terre d'Azile...*160*

Chapter Twelve: The Beauty of Touch **161**

The Origins of Intimacy *165*

Chapter Thirteen: Letting Love In................................**167**

Life's gift..*173*

About the Author **175**

References **177**

Bonus, From Her Next Book: Have We Met?............**178**

Testimonials **182**

My Story About: Who Makes the Bed?

To tell the truth, during my thirties, I was essentially a woman who would not trust deeply enough to go into a committed loving relationship. However, I thought I wanted one, so I did get into a number of short lasting relationships that I am sure I can do another book about. I was always running away at the first signs of conflict. At some point though, I understood that I needed to heal my own issues to be available for a real relationship and I set about working on those issues. By the age of forty, I met him and at forty-four, I married him.

Then, …oooh dear…, surprisingly we both saw that love and healthy sexuality alone was not enough to continue in a loving relationship based in fairness, respect, trust, passion and meaning. We needed much more… ooohhhhh much more…we have very different personalities. Difficult to work together, but possessing a wonderfully wide range of skills between us. Communication was one of our strengths even though I had to express myself in a language that was not my native one, which was tricky. So, Michael had the brilliant idea, on which we agreed, that to create a fairer balance during arguments, I should be encouraged to speak in Spanish. He said he would understand the essential message from my Latino body language and I would be much less frustrated to express myself. This ensured that what each of us was saying was really what we meant. Body language goes a long way in these situations. So, between arguments and fights, Michael learned Spanish with the feeling that I was the best language teacher he had ever had.

Establishing our core values and the interpretation and understanding of them was very dramatic at first, but we went through it slowly and at times fiercely.

In those first weeks living together, after almost four years of long distance Trans-Atlantic relationship, one day, between tears after a fight, we had a good laugh about the subject of WHO MAKES THE BED?

Actually, I love the crisp feeling of freshly laundered sheets, so for me it is very important to change the bedding frequently. Michael is less fussy about that, but feels good about setting up the day in an ordered way by making the bed nicely and tidily. Conclusion, he carefully makes the bed, 'just so', every morning before going downstairs to breakfast and I lovingly change to silky fresh sheets whenever I want. Win-Win solution!

This is what we do in many subjects to deal with the beauties and pains of our differences. We are grateful that the passion of relationship is still with us.

Acknowledgments

Together is better...Relational Capital is one of the most valuable qualities I have and it is manifested in this book.

Together with myself to be free from limitations, together with my late mother and my sister Layla, from where I have my consciousness of love, together with my father who died too soon, for the love stored in me that he gave during those short and precious first three years. Together with my husband Michael, learning every day how to be better partners. Together in our experiences as a couple and therapists, we published a series of articles about Conscious Relationship in 2013 that is the base of this book.

I worked together with dear Marina Nani whom I met in London. She has a huge love for books and has created an organization to help people to write and publish. It was from her the idea of this, my second book, was born. It was Marina who coached us to find the title of the book, therefore she is the God-Mother of this book.

Infinite thanks to Michael, my husband, for his poems and for his patience and loving listening to theories and experiences and for correcting, editing and adding subtle touches to my Spanglish Sentences. To Claire Morley who helped with the eBook.

Thank you to Therese Cafaro for the gift of editing the book. Thanks to Guillermo (Willi) Ricken, for expressing his love through the foreword.

And, finally, together with my clients, working to create success, health and joy in life, thus contributing to a sustainable and more meaningful world.

Thank you all

Foreword

What a joy to write these words!

    Viola, my dear friend and teacher, is one of those rare human beings who treads this earth truly embodying both wisdom and compassion. Such a rare feat! Thus, my unfettered delight upon receiving the surprising invitation to write this foreword to her second book.

    Many, many moons ago, hearing the equally surprising news of Viola's engagement to Michael, whose deep and inspiring poetry you will find enriching these pages, I wrote the following poem:

Two People

*Very dear to my heart, are about to acknowledge their love for
each other, my beloved friends Viola and Michael.
What shall I write you? What shall I say? I am speechless!!
This union, just like life itself, is a complete mystery.
What could I even wish you both?
That your love lasts forever? NO!
That you shall always be happy? NO!
That you shall have smooth sailing? NO!
I have nothing to wish you, for things are as they are.
And yet, just for the fun of it, I can say this:
May life bring you all that it will bring you.
May you humbly accept it ALL.
May you always be surprised, every second of the way.
May you equally embrace all the joys and all the sorrows
with an open, quivering heart.
May you honour the unknown,
For you will never know each other,
For you will never know what's coming.
May you truly never know anything at all!
May you never escape from the present,
May you, together, be warriors of Truth.
May wisdom and compassion always be your guides.
May you see and acknowledge God in each other's eyes.
No matter what.*

Have Viola and Michael had smooth sailing? NO!

Have they always been happy? NO!

Still, no matter what, they have truly embraced all the joys and sorrows their magnificent relationship has bestowed them and based upon their deep work of never escaping the present, this extraordinary book has emerged.

What does it mean to be in a deep, loving, conscious relationship? How does one 'get there'? What is conscious communication and how can we achieve it? What is a healthy sexuality? Here you will find the answers to these and many more questions, written in a clear, helpful prose, by someone who 'walks the talk'.

Offering wonderful pointers and guidelines born of Viola's deep personal experience and vast therapeutic knowledge, *Who Makes the Bed* is for anyone who is in a relationship, or out of a relationship, or starting a relationship, or who simply is dreaming of having one. It is filled not only with extremely valuable information, but, more importantly, with the fearless honesty and the passion to help others discover their essence, that is the hallmark of Viola's work. Love, wisdom and enthusiasm permeate every word within these pages, and every reader, no matter what stage of a relationship they are in, will benefit from them.

Guillermo (Willi) Ricken

Chapter One:
Falling in and Out of Love

Finally, that man or that woman that you have been waiting for, comes bursting in to your life and lights up your senses, floods your body with a rush of adrenaline and hormones and reminds you of the true meaning, the true dimension of the word longing. Reminds you of the intensity that those feelings of desire can attain, desire that is irresistible and so hard to control. Your ego boundaries vanish, you feel so much an indivisible part of the union. You think that together you will be capable of almost anything. You feel ready to devote yourself exclusively to the well-being, the pleasure and the delight of this angel, this being who takes your heart into the fifth dimension.

Bliss state
We call it 'falling in love'. Indeed, the sensation can be very similar to that of falling. You fall into a bliss state. The sun is shining and your worries have disappeared. You are walking on air, the ground no longer solid under your feet, a strong force of attraction is pulling you, accelerating you onward without concern. The scenario is as familiar as life on earth, indeed the survival of the human species has depended on this phenomenon for millions of years. In the traditional 'Fairy Tale' style, the ending of the story would be 'and they rode off in to the sunset' or 'and they lived happily ever after.'

Change in lifestyle
However, our day to day reality tends to be somewhat different from

such romantic dreaming. After the euphoria of that first stage of 'falling', which could last for days or months, the partners will begin to discover the differences in their tastes, their ways of dealing with life as they try travelling together, agreeing on sexual frequency, spending time with each other's friends etc. Living together will help to bring these differences to the surface and, provided there is effective communication, allow them to be discussed and hopefully resolved. Both the partners will then face the task of letting go of their 'I'm free and single' habits and begin creating the new relationship, sharing and living together and making the adjustments and compromises that this entails. We should not underestimate the change in lifestyle created by the transition from 'single' to 'in a relationship'.

Different expectations
Whenever two people come together and create a relationship they will face cultural issues. Very often there will be a wide range of differences in the expectations of the man and woman about how the relationship is going to be. The joyful, vivid, loving passions of their initial encounter can be eroded by these differences, the realities of the relationship. However, it is not the action of living together, nor that of getting married, that suffocates the relationship, but the unconscious engagement into the relationship without the development of effective communication skills between the partners as a means for resolving differences.

Cards on the table, a principal quality of Intimacy
Imagine how helpful it would be, if, early on in a new relationship, partners managed to create a time and space and found the courage to truthfully share their personal weaknesses and expectations of the relationship. What is it that they love about the other and what do they find difficult? What is their pooled list of talents, who will be best at doing what? How will they deal with

sharing money, sharing responsibility for those everyday tasks? The topics are many, but if the differences surface at an early stage, dealing with them will be so much simpler.... but this would be in a perfect world and we have to do the best we can with current reality.

Role models

'Creating a Conscious Relationship' is a rare subject of study on academic curriculums. The 'classroom' on relationships, for most young adults, has been the years of living with parents, grandparents, siblings and other influential family members. Information about how relationships work (or perhaps how they do not work) will have been collected from not only from observation of family role models, conditioning in schools and from their community, but also from romantic stories in literature, the cinema and the television.

Unfamiliar domain

The knowledge of what works and what doesn't, will usually be put together by the partners over the years in a process of trial and error and the progress of this process will often be spiced up by blaming and power games. There are more likely to be 'told you so' judgmental, clumsy comments from some family members, rather than regular access to helpful, balanced insight from wise and impartial friends or from a mentor, relationship coach, psychotherapist or counsellor. Letting go of the old habits, coping with the new surroundings and setting off into this unfamiliar domain of relationship can be a painful experience. Many relationships end in some kind of separation when difficulties cannot be resolved.

Giving, flowing into receiving and developing intimacy

We dream of loving and caring for our partner, of being loved and cared for and appreciated for who we really are. The conscious relationship is one which is filled with conscious acts of love and caring. It is about giving. It develops from a conscious intention to bring joy and contentment into our partner's life. When this dynamic is working both ways, with giving flowing into receiving, the result is the development of a deeply nourishing and harmonious intimacy for both participants.

Daring to explore the boundaries

So, what are the capabilities and the skills that we can develop to help us safely follow that powerful, exciting, sexual attraction and move closer to the situation we are all longing for? Learning from experience is always a powerful pathway, better to be active, daring to explore freely, looking for the boundaries of this new domain, rather than holding back, cautious and hesitant, limited by our fears. By actively searching for knowledge about the dynamics of relationship, we can speed up our learning time and reduce the difficulty of the quest.

Love draws us back, time and again

Recognising the conflicts as learning opportunities as they pop up into the dynamics of the relationship and focusing on understanding the lessons contained in the uncomfortable experiences will help partners develop a deeper understanding of each other. The presence of a strong love and appreciation of the precious value of the relationship will draw the partners back, time and again, to this difficult work.

So, what is the essential content of the Conscious Loving Relationship? What subjects should our learning process include to create the precious harmony of intimacy? Below are seven important aspects contributing to success:-

1-Love
2-Effective Communication
3-Healthy Sexuality
4-Core values held in common
5-Some shared interests and hobbies
6-Agreement on the distribution of duties
7-Continous Learning and Healing

Love's Song

How spins your morning world?
As I feel you across an ocean,
Distant in that peaceful self-made safe space,
Dimmed down, protected by high mirrored walls,
Sheltering from the heat of your desire
Cool and alone, far from my brown body,
The wind of change in your rich chestnut hair.
It scares me to see you withdrawn from longing,
Your loving arms folded across your soft breasts,
Moulding the hurt and the ecstasy into stifled memory,
Dusty and unused, pushed away, unwelcome and dry.
Your brown eyes too sad to feel, flowing with salty tears,
Soft heart abandoned, beyond expectation,
Too tight to open, unwilling to cry.
Vivid image and so lonely,
Not one you might choose to sing about.
But listen to this, hear another song Viola,
For you are beloved, Mo'mina, the one who believes.
I have known you from within, breath warm in my ear.
I have felt your core upon me, squeezed here to my heart.
Come, join my longing, tumble in my tousled thoughts,
Relaxed among words spilling from my lips,
Showered with the love flowing from my heart,
Your body wet and alive, pulsing with quiet acceptance,
hope and belonging deep in your dark eyes.
I know how you love me, and how I adore loving you,
For you have untangled my twisting traumas,
Laid bare my wounds and bathed them in your soul.
My spirit is learning to sing again,
Healed and respected, open and vulnerable.
Hear my song, for I trust you with my heart.

Chapter Two
Love and Intimacy

We have many types of relationships in our lives and here we are choosing to look at what is perhaps the most challenging of them all, the long term, loving, sexual relationship. Building a successful loving relationship out of the chaos of the instinctive, hectic, passions of falling in love will not be a one-night happening. Beyond the myth of the arrow strike of Eros, the evolution of the loving relationship is a steady demanding task that will depend on commitment to love, effective communication and the intimacy of healthy sexuality. The relationship will grow more easily if we hold a number of core values in common, share some interests and hobbies and be able to agree on a fair distribution of the duties of living together. By engaging in continuous learning and healing we can connect with our meaning and inspire others. The paradox is that some of the ways we choose to live our love can also produce quite painful experiences.

Focus on the journey
Wherever we are in our life story, whether we are looking for a new relationship or already involved in a good or not so good one, working to create that conscious loving relationship will be a voyage of discovery where the journey itself is the focus rather than arrival at the destination. Living a loving relationship through the day-to-day happenings and surprises that life produces can be likened to continuous participation in a workshop of personal development. The results we are hoping for will steadily materialise as we develop

awareness and become conscious of what nourishes strong relationship.

Love springs eternal, the favourite surround of Intimacy
True love flows effortlessly from a being who appreciates and is in peace with their inner self. Your capacity to love another is based upon your ability to love and cherish the person you are. The love comes from that home store. That capability will be the foundation of the structure of all your relationships and the foundation of intimacy. Loving yourself, appreciating who you are, will help develop the inner self-confidence, which is the core to being yourself. It takes courage to be true to yourself rather than hoping to deserve love by conforming to a stereotype of goodness, taken on from exterior conditioning. Appreciating and being true to yourself, without the need to play any camouflage personality, will attract those other beings who really appreciate the one you are deep down inside and that natural compatibility will provide the depth that nourishes lasting conscious relationship. Relationships have less surprises waiting in the wings when both partners have been confidently being themselves from their first meeting.

Confidence building
To develop this self-appreciation, we need to create, for ourselves, a truthful picture of our personal strengths and weaknesses. We can then grow into and develop those confidence-building strengths and, by forgiving ourselves the weaknesses, break with the underlying, limiting, beliefs which have created them. This is a challenging journey that will be made easier with the help of a professional therapist or relationship coach.

Learn of love from experience
We sometimes carry a fear to be alone, stemming from our group based origins. This can lead to hanging on to miserable, energy

draining, relationships rather than setting off, solo, into the unknown. Experiment with being by yourself, dare to learn the language of love from personal experience, discover your needs and abilities and develop the capability to give and take. Privilege the growth of the loving relationship with yourself and the self-confidence that makes it easier to relate to others. It is almost impossible to experience deep intimacy with a partner if we have not already created it with ourselves.

Choosing to make love with intimacy

We love because we are attracted by what we perceive and here we are not only talking about love in terms of passion and physical desire. The caring actions of giving love fills us with pleasure. These are moments when we place our partner's joy and contentment high on our list of priorities and this must not be at the cost of neglecting ourselves. We choose to love the other to help them grow and to build the needed self-confidence to be true to themselves. There is no underlying motive present to change the way they are, the love is not given in exchange for some expected return, but simply because to do so creates in us a wonderful sensation of fulfilment.

For the receiver, the feeling of being loved simply for who you are brings deep nourishment to the psyche. The unconditional care received amplifies the emotions of joy and happiness. Intimacy appears and grows into the space left by the departure of mental camouflage. It flourishes when the defences are let down, it develops when there is nothing left to hide.

The passion and desire that are the elements of sexual intercourse are the products of two loving, giving spirits engaged in pleasuring the other. This is the 'making' of love. Love grows strongly in the intimacy of moments when we are focused on its giving, as flowers will grow to great beauty when they receive water and appreciation every day.

It is important to realize that the converse is also true. The moment that we begin to focus on what we feel is wrong or disappointing about our partner is the moment that those characteristics will begin to grow disproportionally important in our minds.

Assume responsibility

The will to change comes from within. You cannot hope to change your partner's negative behaviour patterns by complaining and scolding them, though in our humanity, sometimes those actions are inevitable. Rather, be concerned with developing loving presence toward yourself and becoming aware of your needs and your negative patterns. Work to understand where they have come from and let them go. Assume responsibility for transforming your own behaviour patterns. If you can be modelling the behaviour and walking the talk, you can help your partner to become conscious of their habits and help both of you to develop other, more positive, behaviour. By assuming responsibility for their own behaviour and its contribution to the conflicts and disagreements, each of the partners can contribute to the growth and the intimate harmony of the conscious relationship.

Ask for help

In a way, all of us are involved in the subject of relationship. Some are looking for a new love relationship, some are working to improve an existing relationship, and some are deciding if they stay or if they leave the relationship. Some are trying to get out of their relationship and some others are working to get over the last relationship, or to be open to the next one. In all these cases, it is possible to include consciousness, hope and meaning. You can also consult a relationship coach or specialised psychotherapist to work on the process together, helping you to be more centred, fair and efficient. Often this will create a shorter, simpler and less painful process.

Owning what has always been mine

What would it be to accept the crossing of our two paths?
An incident so normal on any day of this magic Earth.
Breathing naturally without yearning for more,
Simply conscious and without expectation.

Soaked in the clarity of happiness
Feeling the pull towards situations that generate bliss.
The choice inevitably leaves me vulnerable, defenceless,
Grateful and ready for meetings of this kind.

For the joy is already within me,
The love that fills this strong heart, truly mine.
It is I who is aware of this bliss.

Every day as we spin around our star
If I will listen, if I care to hear,
The enchanting song of this life awaits me.

Who Makes the Bed?

Chapter Three:
The Flow of Communication

Conscious relationships can be likened to a seed that is carefully planted in good earth. The gardener is aware and has created favourable conditions before starting his work. Likewise, a couple's relationship, situated in the sunshine of the truth, cared for with respect, watered with love and encouraged with communication, will grow on strong roots and produce many beautiful flowers and fruits. Mutual love develops its strength in the presence of intimacy and trust, so the picture we give of ourselves and the one we receive from our partner needs to be clear and truthful, a faithful representation. By daring to paint an open and accurate picture of ourselves that communicates the colours of our strengths, as well as the shadows of our weaknesses, we plant ourselves and the relationship in a rich and fertile earth.

Communication capital
Communication is a process of exchange of information. Success requires contact, connection, channels, content, transmission and reception and, above all, understanding. However, if we were to compare communication in the couple relationship with the data exchanging operation between a mobile and a laptop, we would be giving a very shallow example of the rich depth and the variety of communication that we, as intelligent multi-talented beings, are capable of. The loving relationship brings into contact the differing yet complementary character traits of masculine and feminine energy. This tricky connection is simplified and reinforced by clear

communication. Partners have different perceptions, but by co-operating and collaborating, exchanging knowledge, ideas and a variety of opinions, by sharing love, pleasure and intimate feelings, by organising tasks and looking for harmony and agreement in a climate of tolerance, they will have a broader range of talents and a richer choice of solutions. The same two partners, suspicious and resentful and in continuous competitive conflict with each other to retain control, will turn their relationship into an energy-draining nightmare.

Communication channels
Our body senses and organs provide us with many different ways to communicate. We can talk and listen, using our mouths and ears, exchanging information whispering words or speaking, more crudely shouting with noises, grunts, crying or moaning, our ears picking up obvious or subtle information from inflections or a tone of voice. We are tactile and can use touch to connect, passing affection and tender feelings without words, using many different parts of our bodies, giving and receiving, exchanging exquisite (or brutal) energy through contact between our sensitive and sensual skins. The way we breathe transmits a multitude of information on the calmness or excitation of our body state and this can be seen and heard. We inhale enticing aromas, body smells and exhale sighs of relaxation. We sweat, exuding body odour. We can use our eyes to read written words or perceive visual media and also to decipher signals from body gestures such as happy smiles, emotional tears, displeased frowns, bored yawns, embarrassed looks or impatient drumming fingers and the more instinctive body language such as hair standing on end, shocked gasps or the holding of breath. All these gestures when decoded carry messages and perhaps the most subtle of these communication channels is the use of intuition.

Unconscious learning

As children, we imitate many of these communication techniques, picking them up through observation of our principle role models, our parents, families and teachers. Children learn well through imitating, accurately mirroring the behaviour and body language of their role models and they learn and use these skills unconsciously without realising the sources. Unfortunately for the children, when the parents themselves have grown up in a family where communication was troubled or dysfunctional, the set of skills that are passed on to them can be quite twisted or negatively biased. So, in some cases, as young adults, we will dive into the adventure of a loving relationship with a poorly suited range of communicational skills that will need some refinement if the relationship is to succeed.

How well do I communicate?

Improving communicational skills will begin with creating a picture of how we ourselves manage to communicate. What are our strengths and our weaknesses? Are we in touch with our feelings? Can we express the tenderness of our love through our sexuality and talk easily about ourselves? Is it easy to ask for what we need? Do we have the courage to say no when it is necessary? This inner picture will help to boost our self-confidence and highlight the areas where we need to improve our skills. We can focus on knowing ourselves better by working with a therapist and bringing into our consciousness intimate and unexpressed feelings.

Building up our awareness helps us to acknowledge and value our qualities, helps us to let go of self-defensive habits and, with the help of intimacy, share our deepest feelings to a trusted partner. In-depth communication with another requires courage and practice.

Trust and truth

Trust is a bonding element in relationships, it holds the partners together, giving time for misunderstandings to be cleared away. When there is difference of opinion, healthy communication helps to prevent development of the conflict. Opinions can be expressed and owned safely if there is no fight to convert the opinion of the other. Accepting to differ is a mature acknowledgment of the other's individuality. Hearing a truth can hurt the ego but denying the truth will damage the soul and then the rebuilding of trust takes time and much work. When we realise that we are mistaken, the sooner we move out of denial, apologise and communicate our regret, the less the damage caused. Insisting on our innocence or on being right, when that is not the case, will be temporarily good for our ego but will end by undermining our credibility, devaluing all the other things that we say. Being able to trust in oneself and in the truth of what your partner says is essential, for non-manipulative communication really nourishes relationship and opens up the pathway to intimacy.

Knowing by heart
When two people meet and begin an open-hearted, loving relationship they are creating a private, intimate world of continuous communication about what is really going on within the relationship. There is a profound exchange of sensitive information about themselves. The two hearts, sensitive and defenceless, will hide nothing from each other. They will know each other by heart. Naked and unashamed, they will share their intimacy with pleasure and love. They will verbalise fears and worries as they express hopes and frustrations and their dreams and their pains. Caring communication involves a running process of feedback within the relationship. The couple dares to share to this extent because they trust in the support of their partner and know they too are trusted. Conscious communication facilitates the encounter between the bodies and the spirits of the partners, preparing the solid foundations of deep intimacy.

Expression and reception

A flow of information requires both expression and reception and to become a successful flow, the communication will depend on truthful expression and receptive awareness. Truthful expression can take many forms such as talking, touching, gesturing and loving and the closer these forms come to expressing the essence of the person involved, the more powerful will be the action. Receptive awareness of spoken words will be listening to hear what is really being said, uncovering the needs concealed among the words and between the lines. Awareness to touch will awaken the body's senses, opening up the spirit to receive the energy expressed in the contact. Observing gestures will facilitate translating the body's language into coherent information. Receptive awareness of love will be sensing the love being offered and opening the heart to let love in. Awareness of emotional expression will be through understanding, feeling empathy and deepening emotional connection.

Conflict resolution

Probably the most prolific channel of communication between two partners in a loving relationship will be the exchange of spoken words. Most of our conflicts (and the conflict resolution) will be built up around what is said. It follows that if we wish to get better at resolving our conflicts or preventing conflicts from developing, we should pay much more attention to what we say and how we say it. Our awareness in listening will focus on hearing what is really being said to us and how best to acknowledge what we have heard. Both actions require presence, practice, motivation and restraint.

Creating deeper connections

Imagine being able to transform those perpetual family conflicts into opportunities for creating deeper and more loving connections with your partner or your children. What if you could enter into a conversation with your partner confident that you would be really heard, rather than reluctant to speak at all, for fear that everything you say would be misconstrued?

Conditioned to conflict

Marshall Rosenberg, the founder of Non-Violent Communication (NVC), explains below, why it is so difficult for us to experience that kind of success in our communications.

'Most of us have been educated from birth to compete, judge, demand and diagnose, to think and communicate in terms of what is 'right' and 'wrong' with people. We express our feelings in terms of what another person has 'done to us.' We struggle to understand ourselves, what it is that we want or need in the moment, and how to effectively ask for what we want or need without using unhealthy demands, threats or coercion. So many of us struggle every day to share what we feel or what we want in a way that can really be heard. We simply haven't been taught the effective communication skills, emotional vocabulary, or self-awareness needed to get 'unstuck' in those challenging moments, or to prevent those moments from happening in the first place.'

Non-violent communication

Marshall Rosenberg formulated a process, which he called Non-Violent Communication, to help us resolve existing conflicts and prevent differing viewpoints from developing into conflict.

His process is founded on transforming the way that I 'express' myself and the way that I 'listen'. While listening before talking, I will 'observe' the situation to see what is going on. When I talk, I will be trying to express clearly how 'I am', without blaming or criticising anyone else. I can say what I observe, hear or imagine etc. and I can then say how these observations make me 'feel' (I feel scared, offended, joyful, irritated, frustrated, etc.). Based on these feelings, I will then know what 'I need' or value, finishing with a 'clear request' of actions that I would like taken. This request will be centred on what we would like the other person to do in order 'to enrich my life or the lives of both of us'.

While I am making the statement consisting on the four components above, the person listening to me is receiving these same four components and when I have finished will connect back to me.

The other aspect of effective communication consists of me receiving from the other person (if it is possible) these same four components. If is not possible for any reason, then I, in my empathetic connection with them, would already have perceived what they 'observe, feel, need', and at that point, I invite them to simply make a request of what they need, discovering then what will 'enrich their lives' as I hear the 'request' that they formulate in reply.

True needs

Before a couple's journey into non-violent communication begins, a subject will probably not be opened up for discussion until one of the partners is frustrated, upset and emotional. The beginning of the exchange can be full of anger, empty of hope and typified by statements like 'I can't take any more of this.' There may be verbal aggression and insults and these will have to be listened to in attentive silence in order to allow the root cause of the frustration to appear. If, instead of listening, the partner mounts a counter attack, there will be no one left listening and effective communication breaks down. The frustrated partner needs to feel they are really being heard. Their true needs will emerge from the process when given the place and the invitation. The listener must work hard to transform the upsurge of their feelings of judgment and criticism into meaningful expressions of empathetic understanding and connection.

A fluid dance

All these techniques we are writing about are not only applicable to the use of words. The conscious and receptive attitudes involved can also be conveyed through the medium of silence, simple presence, facial expression and body language. Whatever the channels of communication being used, the partners can learn to dance with the different forms, transforming passivity into action, finding the fluidity to weave their way between moments of expression and moments of receptivity, developing awareness by listening and observing, unravelling the tangles of confusion, loosening the knots that restrain the expression of emotions, awakening the body senses and opening the heart to let love in. When communication between the partners is working well, the conscious dance may begin because both partners are fully present and participating. Couples have different perceptions, but by co-operating and collaborating, exchanging knowledge, ideas and a variety of opinions, by sharing love, pleasure and intimate feelings, by organising tasks and looking for harmony and agreement in a climate of tolerance, the two partners will have a broader range of talents and a richer choice of solutions.

Between two souls.

Together afterwards,
Immersed in a comforting stillness
Populated only by her presence and mine,
I recall the sweet taste of her kisses,
Savouring the glowing energy of love,
The nourished longing of our hearts.
We rest intertwined, breathing softly,
Listening to echoes of expressed emotions
That float between the moments of emptiness
Drifting among unspoken words
Of a silent conversation

Who Makes the Bed?

Chapter Four
Paradigms and Limiting Thought Habits: 'The Personal Law'

Note: when I was reviewing the second edition of Who makes the Bed? I decided to include this chapter of my book "Breathing the Rhythm of Success" (1999). Following the detailed exercises of this chapter will bring more clarity and improve your relationship with yourself and others, enabling communication in a flowing and influential manner.

I love this story about Michelangelo. It is said when asked how he went about creating a sculpture, he replied that the statue already existed inside the marble. He claimed that God had already created 'Moses' and 'La Pieta' and his work was to merely get rid of the excess marble around what was God's creation.

There is a divine essence or spark in all of us and we get to see it, recognise it and feel it at certain times in our lives. It is a sensation of expansion, celebration, stability, the love of life itself. In our daily lives, we forget this sensation of divine essence. Yet we reconnect with it at specific moments such as on seeing your own newly born child, or when you fall in love, or when you are transported by creative inspiration, or when we go beyond ourselves to commit a truly heroic act. In moments such as these, we act and come into close contact with our essence.

Carl G. Jung formulated the idea of the 'collective unconscious', a structural layer of the human psyche that 'contains the whole spiritual heritage of mankind's evolution'. He claimed that there is a 'collective psychic substratum' deep in the mind that is 'born anew in the brain structure of every individual'. Rebirthing/Breathwork takes this idea one step further in the realisation that we are all part of an essence that is one and the same at this profound level. The concept of Divine Mind suggests that we are not only identical in our core, but that we are basically all one with the same Being.

It can thus be said that we are all gifted with natural talents, knowledge and numerous different attributes. Around our true essence, however, we build up an increasingly sophisticated 'belief system' from the moment of conception, at birth and during the first few years of life, all the way through to the present day. This belief system is made up of positive and negative thoughts. The positive thoughts are aligned with the nature of our true essence whereas the negative ones limit us in everyday life regardless of all our wishes and efforts to change. These negative thoughts disconnect and separate us from our essence and a dense mass begins to form around God's great sculpture. They create a rift between our essence and us, they limit our existence and they give form to and shape the 'ego'.

Belief Systems

When I refer to 'ego' in this context, I am referring to the false idea that we each have of ourselves. The ego is merely an illusion although it is one that exerts a very powerful influence over us.

'As a man thinks in his heart, so is he' (Proverbs 23:7) is an expression that takes in not only all of one's being but also all of the circumstance in one's life. *A man is literally what he thinks and his character is the total of all of his thoughts.* In the same way that a plant sprouts forth from a seed and cannot come into existence without one, so a person's every action originates from the hidden seeds of thought and could not exist without them. This can be applied to both spontaneous and non-premeditated actions in addition to those that are deliberate.

'Action is the flowering of thought and both joy and suffering are its fruits; for this reason, a man reaps the sweetness and the bitterness of his own harvest' (adapted from Allen, 1903).

Your belief system forms the basis for how you see the world and it is ultimately the source of your behaviour and attitude to life. We tend to think that we see things objectively the way that they are, yet it's not really like that. What happens is that we see the world, not as the world is, but as the result of what we think we are. When you use words to describe what you see, you are really describing yourself, together with how you perceive things and your belief system. According to the model used in Rebirthing, this limiting aspect of our belief system is known as 'I believe' and consists of a false image that we each have of ourselves.

'As a man thinks in his heart, so is he.' (Proverbs 23:7)

'We are what we think and whatever we are emerges through our thoughts. We construct the world with our thoughts.' (Adapted from Buddha)

'The wholeness of the human being means that our behaviour is revealed through our actions and thoughts. Thoughts and actions are thus one of the same substance and can be interpreted and transferred from one level to the other'. (Dr Fritz Perls)

The path to developing in an integrated way is composed of focusing deeply within your feelings and thought and outwards to the infinite.

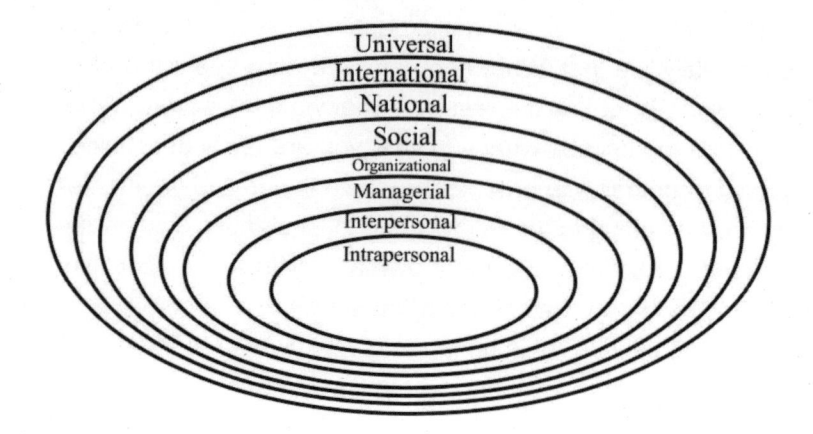

```
Universal
International
National
Social
Organizational
Managerial
Interpersonal
Intrapersonal
```

As I mentioned previously, we are not generally aware of the countless positive and negative thoughts that go to make up our belief system.

Remember that instead of having what you want, you get what you think.

All things are created twice; there is the mental or first creation, and a physical or second creation to all things. Whether you are aware of it or not, that first creation exists in every area of your life and the second creation, which is you yourself, is either the result of your own pro-active plan or of your fears and apprehensions, together with the circumstances and habits that you have acquired from the past.

THE ICEBERG PRINCIPLE (simple)

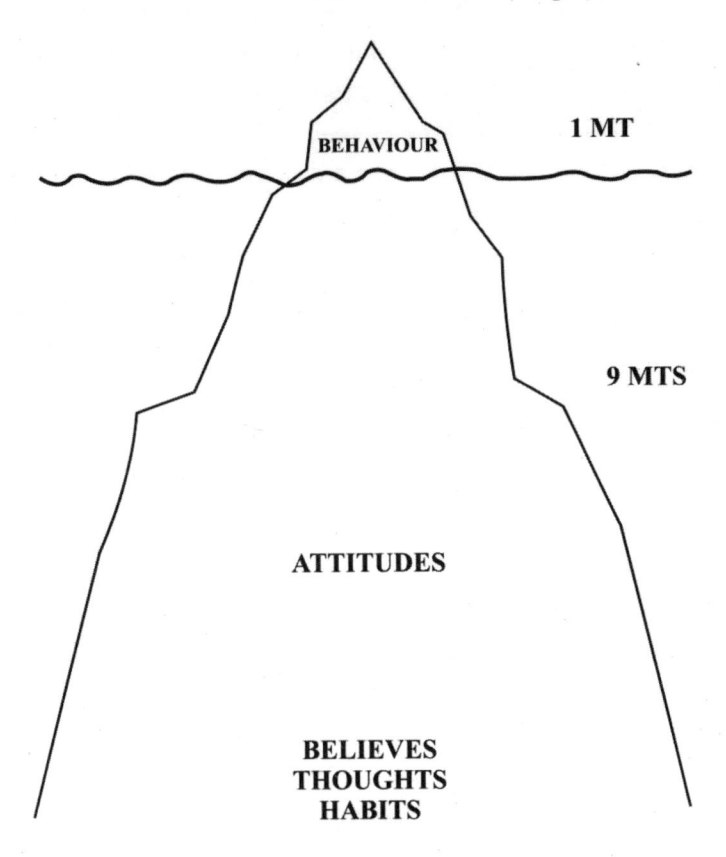

BEHAVIOUR

1 MT

9 MTS

ATTITUDES

BELIEVES
THOUGHTS
HABITS

For every metre of an iceberg that can be seen floating above the surface of the water, there are nine metres that cannot be seen below it. People are like icebergs in that, to transform our behaviour (i.e. the 'visible' result that is above the surface), we must first work on ourselves at a deeper level or down around the 9-metre mark, which is where the thought patterns and beliefs that form the basis of our attitude towards life and lead us to express ourselves with one form of behaviour or another are to be found.

'Man is made or unmade by himself; in the armoury of thought he forges the weapons by which he destroys himself; he also fashions the tools with which he builds for himself heavenly mansions of joy and strength and peace. By the right choice and true application of thought, man ascends to the Divine Perfection; by the abuse and wrong application of thought, he descends below the level of the beast. Between these two extremes are all the grades of character, and man is their maker and master.' (Allen, 1903)

Why the thought? The mind is the most powerful instrument that man possesses and, as science has proven; it works non-stop twenty-four hours a day (unless it can be trained not to do so). Thought is energy that moves continuously and true to the Universal Laws of Thought, it is fundamental in creating the world within and around us, physically, emotionally, mentally and spiritually speaking.

Anything that you repeatedly think about ends up coming true for you and 'whatever the mind resists, persists' in your own personal life. The desire to change is unfortunately not enough on its own. Just take a minute to think about your own life. How many times have you feared that something was going to happen and then it has come true? Afterwards you probably said, 'I knew that was going to happen'. However, as you learn to consciously and intentionally direct your mind to be attentive, your energy moves in a more continuous way and you begin to experience more integration within yourself.

At this point, you probably start to recognise the enormous amount of negative ideas and thoughts that you have about yourself, about life, love, relationships, money, success, etc. It's all a very personal story, along with everything else that has been stuffed down at the psychological 9-metre mark: the way you were born, your first breath, the first few years of your life, how you were brought up, your family's beliefs and cultural beliefs in general, and above all, how you yourself perceive your life story.

'I am a co-creator'. We are all co-creators by way of our thoughts. All things are quite literally one. Everything is interconnected. The universe is pure energy, everything in it is energy (this fact is recognised by quantum physics) and existence itself is also made of this same fundamental substance. The energy that interconnects everything in the universe shapes human consciousness as well and it responds in an incredible way to our thoughts and feelings. Our energy, in the form of thoughts and feelings, irradiates outwards to the world, affecting other energy systems as it does so. Gary Zukav has expressed it in the following way: 'In a strict mathematical as well as a philosophical sense, whatever is out there would seem to depend on what we decide here inside. Modern physics states that an observer cannot observe something without altering what he is observing'.

So, if you decide to undertake a process of personal growth, you first need to ascertain and examine what is going on inside of yourself, because that is where all of your life circumstances are created.

Sublime experiences can occur even in the face of a difficult situation, when something deep down inside you, tells you how valuable you are and how wonderful life can be. Listen to what is going on deep down inside of yourself. You can return to the essential being that you really are and expand this outward. Cherish the divine personal motivation within yourself and use it to achieve complete success.

Knowing yourself
'Knowing oneself is the beginning of wisdom and the end of fear.' (Adapted from Krishnamurti)

The greatest journey that you can make is by entering into your heart and discovering yourself. Getting to know yourself is a voyage of personal growth, of understanding your behaviour, your different moods, relationships and encounters with others. It is the discovery of who you really are as a complete being. Allowing yourself to observe your fears and transcend your limitations will set you free and contentment will be almost impossible for you without this knowledge.

The process of getting to know yourself will lead you through important changes in your life and provide you with the opportunity of discovering who you really are. By working on yourself and constantly observing your thoughts, feelings and actions, you will discover that, behind all of the perceptions and projections of your mind, there is a being filled with light and wisdom who can transcend all forms of limitation.

The Personal Law*:

(*The term of Personal Lie was originated by Leonard Orr and Sondra Ray, see their book 'Rebirthing in the new age, later on it became Personal Law).

Of all the precious truths pertaining to the soul that have been retrieved and brought to light in this Age, none is more joyous or so full of divine promise and hope than the fact that man is the master of his own thoughts, the shaper of his own personality and the maker of his own situation and destiny. As a being of power, intelligence and love, he is master over his own thoughts. Man, himself is the key to every situation and he possesses within himself the power to transform, regenerate and make of himself whatever he desires.

An endless stream of thoughts goes through our minds like a never-ending film. Scientific research has shown that the mind has somewhere between 80,000 and 300,000 different thoughts every day. 'The constant chatter of the mind is an obstacle in the path of meditation. You can't sit in silence for even a minute without the mind starting to chatter. Thoughts keep flowing, whether they are relevant or irrelevant, whether they make sense or not, there is a constant flow of mind traffic.' (adapted from Osho)

A contribution made by Rebirthing (also known as Breathwork or Conscious Connected Breathing) to this research is the acknowledgement that 80% of all thoughts get repeated over and over again until we believe them, and remember that believing is creating. Thought is creative and it is so powerful that we always create what we believe. This concept becomes quite subtle if we take the results of other research, which shows that 78% of our thoughts are negative and 22% are positive and that is in the best of cases (i.e. Amongst those not having consciously worked with and developed the creative ability of thought). It is sad to think that it's our negative thoughts that get repeated more often! No wonder we get the results that we do and that the world is in the state that it is today.

One aspect of your belief system is your hurt inner child. Therapist Ron Kutz centres directly on 'inside material' when applying his Haikaní therapy system. He maintains that this material gets organised as an internal experience in the following way: Our inside material, which is made up of our very first feelings, beliefs and memories, forms as a response to the stress caused by our surroundings during childhood'. This material may be illogical and primitive but for the helpless, vulnerable child, the conclusions drawn at that time were essential to survival.

Once the inside material is formed, it creates a kind of lens or filter through which all new experiences are viewed. This explains why some people continually choose to live out the same kind of destructive emotional relationships time and time again and why life for others is an on-going trauma and why the majority of us don't manage to learn from our mistakes.

Freud called this urge to repeat the past 'the repetition impulse', while a term for it in contemporary therapy is 'the logic of absurdity'. It is logical when you understand how this inner material shapes your life. It's like seeing everything through rose-coloured glasses (you see everything tinted according to the colour of the lens).

The hypnotherapist Milton Erickson believes that everyone has his or her own individual view of the world or an unconscious inner belief system that acts as a kind of hypnotic trance. It is obvious, therefore, that if you want to change your life, you will have to change your inside material (your glasses).

'I now understand that when a child's development is held back, or when emotions such as anger and pain are repressed, the result will be an adult harbouring an angry, hurt inner child. This child will unconsciously contaminate the behaviour of the adult. It may seem absurd at first that a small child continues to live in an adult's body, but I believe that this hurt and abandoned inner child from our past is the main source of all human misery. Such a presence will continue to contaminate life until the adult manages to reclaim and truly nurture their own inner child.' (Bradshaw, 1992)

Man is always his own master, even during his times of greatest weakness and when he feels abandoned. In those moments of weakness and decline, however, it is the unconscious mind that governs the house and governs it badly. Relaxing into the condition that you find yourself in and assiduously searching for the underlying laws that govern your being will give you the self-control and wisdom to astutely direct your energy and apply your thoughts to more productive matters. This is the conscious master and the individual can only become such a master by discovering within him or herself the laws that govern thought. Such a discovery can only be made by applying oneself and through self-analysis and experience.

Digging deeply into the mine of the soul shows that each one of us has a huge number of negative beliefs, all of them the result of our individual life history. This personal belief system as a whole is known as I BELIEVE. Amongst all of these beliefs there is one group that affects us to a much greater extent and within this group there is one belief, which is the root of all others. This root belief is repeated so many times that it ends up becoming a LAW.

This recurring negative belief is known as the PERSONAL LAW or PERSONAL LIE in Rebirthing/Breathwork. Due to the fact that thought is creative, the constant unconscious repetition of this negative thought makes it come true. This is why it is known as a law. It is, however, a great big lie that negates the true nature of one's being because it is an idea that is totally individual and based on one's own life history and how one interprets what that is. Two people can experience the same event although each one, even in the case of twins, will experience it differently and they will both come to entirely different conclusions and create different laws or none at all. It is not the experience that affects us but our interpretation of the experience.

Any incident or event could be behind the origin of your personal law and it may even have been formed during gestation or at birth. It is not the origin that is most important, however, but the belief itself. For example, if you were an unwanted or illegitimate child, your law could be 'I'm not wanted'. Because thought is creative, you will then go on to unconsciously create circumstances in your life that make you feel 'not wanted' over and over again. The personal law is the cornerstone of the negative belief system that creates the ego. As long as it remains undetected, your personal law works away on an unconscious level and you will be totally unaware of it. If someone's personal law is 'I'm not capable' or 'I'm not up to it', he or she may well decide unconsciously that they are 'not capable' and can become virtually 'useless' in many areas of their life.

The mind also creates another group of beliefs on a subconscious level in order to conceal the personal law from the people around us. If your law is 'I'm not capable', you will be relentlessly trying to demonstrate the opposite (I AM very capable). Trying to impress others with how capable you are and pretending to be capable in general will only create struggle and exhaustion and be a waste of energy. It is, in reality, unnecessary to pretend that you are capable because human beings are naturally born with this attribute. This alternative belief system with which we unconsciously surround our essential being, is known as I PRETEND.

Both systems (I believe and I pretend) are a negation of our essential being or true Self. As human beings, we have all been blessed with attributes, virtues and natural talents. Our perception of external situations, however, leads us to surround ourselves with a layer of negative belief systems that is so strong, we must struggle and exhaust ourselves creating yet another layer on top to conceal it. This vicious circle terminates with us pretending to be what we believe we're not and ignoring what we really are.

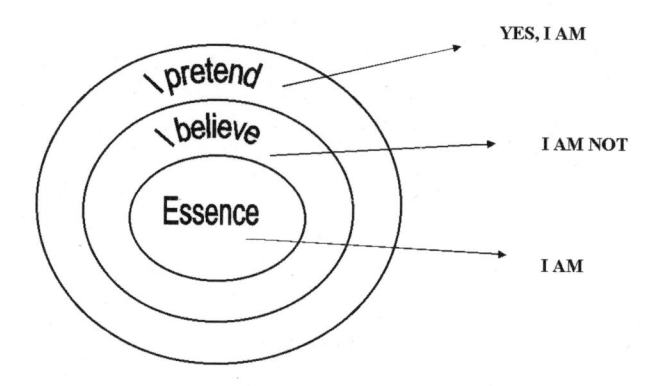

Diagram: Three concentric circles labeled (from outer to inner) "pretend", "believe", and "Essence", with arrows pointing to "YES, I AM", "I AM NOT", and "I AM" respectively.

In this eloquent passage, Tagore refers to the falseness of I BELIEVE and I PRETEND: 'He, whom I confine in my name, is crying in some dungeon. I am always busy building a wall around me; while this wall ascends to Heaven day by day; I lose sight in its shadow of my truthful being. I am proud of this great wall and enhance it with dust and sand, fearing the slightest hole that may appear in my name but in spite of all my care, I lose sight of my truthful being'.

Laws that accompany the Personal Law:

Thought is creative and you are the thinker.

The universe rearranges itself to adapt to the way that you perceive reality. Your thoughts, beliefs and expectations produce results in the physical world. Negative thoughts, together with beliefs in the confining limitation of life, will generate a group of ineffective actions which will end up creating negative results, whereas positive thoughts and positive beliefs about the unlimited possibilities of life produce focus, creative and constructive actions which are more likely to lead to positive results.

The problem is that many of the negative thoughts that create our experience of personal reality are unconscious. The majority of those thoughts are conclusions based on a mistaken perception at some point a long time ago and are in fact neither appropriate nor real. Those Negative thoughts unfortunately often produce results that we don't want.

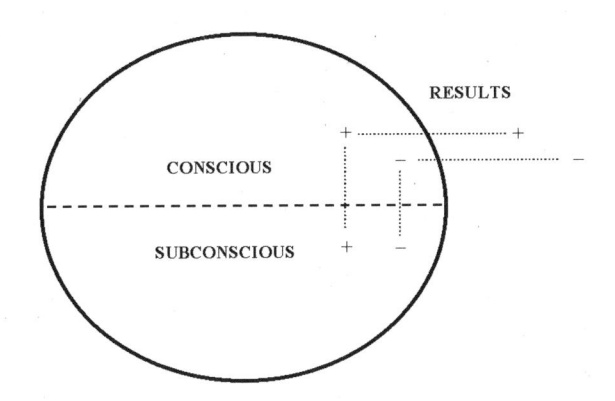

```
                                    RESULTS
                              + ............... +
          CONSCIOUS            - ..................... −
      --------------------------
          SUBCONSCIOUS      +   −
```

One frequently comes into contact with thoughts and beliefs of this kind in a Rebirthing/Breathwork session. With your Rebirther's/Breathworker's support, you can gradually transform them so that they stop producing undesirable results in your life. Most people who have had experience with Rebirthing/Breathwork find that their intuition naturally becomes more enhanced as their mind, body and emotions become clearer. By transforming your limiting thoughts and belief patterns, you find that your outlook on life changes and it is the nature of this outlook that is the foundation of human behaviour.

In other words, the universe appears to say 'yes' to everything you believe. If you believe that people hurt you, you will constantly find yourself in situations where people seemingly hurt you and do you harm. On the other hand, if your belief is that people are in essence good and loving and that they support you, you can experience this instead. We will select the set of facts that confirm our belief system.

If you are not master over the power of your mind, you will feel like a victim whose mind is programmed with the thoughts and beliefs of other people (your parents, teachers, friends, T.V, Media, the press and advertising, etc.).

Your real-life situation will reflect whatever you believe to be true. A simple way of understanding this is to think of there being two parts to the mind:

The Thinker and the Checker.

The 'thinker' does the thinking and the 'checker' puts the evidence together to show that whatever the thinker is thinking is true. It does this by gathering supportive evidence of any kind of belief that you may have about your life experience or your interpretation of it.

The checking part of the mind uses the Laws of Attraction, Projection/Perception/Interpretation and Manifestation/Transformation to do this.

The Law of Attraction: You draw into your life everything that matches and fits in with your belief system.

The Law of Projection/Perception/Interpretation: You interpret everything in accordance with your belief system, regardless of whether anyone else interprets it in the same way or not. You interpret everything you see and experience exactly the way you expect to see or experience it. This process is often based on past experience so this is how you perceive reality. This way of perceiving and interpreting things becomes so much a part of you and so powerful that you project it onto others.

The Law of Manifestation/Transformation: People and/or situations in your life that don't fit in with your beliefs and expectations will either stop being a part of your life or be 'transformed' so that they can conform. This is because you unconsciously create situations that bring up the behavioural patterns in others that serve to reconfirm your law.

Rebirthing/Breathwork is a forceful way of contacting and reclaiming your own individual power. 'Inspiration' means 'the drawing in of breath'. As you breathe in more vitality (Chi/Prana/Ki) using improved breathing patterns and let go of the negativity that you have been holding on to from the past, you naturally open up on an intuitive level, becoming more sensitive and developing a new awareness of both your spirituality and your ability to experience higher levels of consciousness. It is all a matter of becoming aware of the hold that your past has on you and renouncing that hold. This inner process opens you up to a more profound experience of who you really are and gradually brings you in line with the true meaning of your purpose in life.

The Realm of the Emotions:
Ranging from euphoria to tranquillity, emotions are natural and intuitive and they form part of man's multidimensional consciousness.

We are so frightened of others finding out what we really think about ourselves that we become masters of control and struggle. When this thought came to me, I realised, 'Of course, we are masters of something, albeit of inhibiting ourselves'. Being a true master of something, however, means using the talents, virtues and abilities that are natural to us as human beings. So, what happened? Where did we mistake the meaning of mastery? These questions led me to begin to unravel the realm of the emotions.

At what point in our lives did we let the ego turn virtue into vice and what was the incident or event that caused this?

If we start with this premise, then it must be that before everything else there was virtue. Our natural attributes and talents, given the positive space to develop, are what essentially predominate in all of us, together with wisdom and unlimited intelligence.

Making a list of all of our attributes would be endless; Love, patience, intuition, steadfastness, solidarity, memory, versatility, integration, quality, passion, perseverance, contemplation, reflection, tolerance, trust, hope, faithfulness, discipline, generosity, sense of justice, reliability, honesty, politeness, diligence, the ability to express oneself, sensibility, eternal search, creativity, etc. etc. However, while we all possess them all, certain attributes stand out more in some people than in others. The important thing to know is which of your qualities are the outstanding ones amongst all the natural talents that you have been gifted with.

These natural talents can be rediscovered in a number of ways.

One of them is by acknowledging what we like most about ourselves or those characteristics that have been your most efficient allies in times of difficulty and which are the most effective when you express your creativity. Just think about this and then ask yourself: What have I been doing with these attributes? Why aren't they active in all areas of my life? Then, follow the process of self-enquiry, which is the key to understanding your emotions.

If you can't recognise your natural talents by way of your attributes, maybe because of some emotional tie, try isolating the emotions that are limiting you. Ask yourself 'What are the emotions that limit me most?' or 'How do I express my fears and pain?'

I've found that fear is the source of every negative, limiting emotion; the fear of something or the fear that something will happen. It's always fear! So where did the fear come from? There are many answers that range from the collective unconscious to the moment of conception, from gestation in the womb, to birth (the separation from our initial 'aquatic' environment and from one's mother), from the first time that we felt separate from God, to experiences in our childhood or because of deep primal memories.

It is still not known whether this is due to one or several of these factors. What is known, however, is that a profound memory of separation and loneliness accompanies us all through life and forces us to combat fear by building a multiple defence system in order to survive.

Given that there must be an origin to everything, what existed before the fear? Which 'element' got transformed into fear by the 'alchemist'?

Are you familiar with the expression, 'The ego is a great architect for it builds vice out of virtue'? (Adapted from Swami Chidvilasananda 'Gurumayi')

So which virtue did the ego use to create fear? **The sense of self-protection or the instinct for survival** that all living beings possess!

When I discovered this myself, it was like a miracle had happened. All of a sudden, I realised that there is nothing bad in me, not even my fears! Everything is built on goodness, on virtues and attributes and upon 'holy ground'. I finally and clearly understood the meaning of 'free will' and how to develop it.

As all people are different and all of us are unique, how do we each express our fear and why is there a difference? And this is how I created the theory of The Alchemy of Emotions.

If ego (that part of myself that limits me) transformed a virtue of mine into a vice, way back at the beginning of time, then because of my infinite intelligence I can use my imagination and awareness to learn from this same fact. **By following the principles of alchemy whereby elements are separated into base elements, I can go back to the basic and fundamental element, which is THE PURENESS OF ATTRIBUTE**.

There are many negative, limiting emotions and there are numerous ways that they can affect us. Fear, anger, malice, sadness, sorrow, gloom, obsession, hatred, resentment, loneliness, feeling abandoned, grief, anxiety, vengeance, guilt, jealousy, feeling victimised, the list is almost endless. Each one causes a result to manifest in our lives. Joy, gratitude and contentment which are so fundamental for good health and feeling up to par, may be missing from life. The inability to make decisions or face responsibilities and the lack of will power are all so fundamental for getting things done. Mulling things over too much, transforms into worry and obsession, which then limits our ability to genuinely express success.

In the same way that we have predominant attributes, we also have predominant limiting emotions. People experience and express anger in different ways, which doesn't mean to say that we don't all experience it. How a person expresses him or herself emotionally will depend on their predominating emotion. For example, if the predominating emotion is sadness, every time the person feels emotional (and this could be the result of anger, fear or any other emotion), he/she will manifest this in a characteristically sad way. Likewise, if the predominating emotion is anger, every time that they get frightened or sad, they will express this with anger.

This happens because the ego uses our predominant attributes to build up a 'vice', or rather the negative expression of the given attribute. The ego gets our attributes to turn against us, instead of having them work for us. We do have the ability, however, to change this result.

Our attributes are our best and most loyal servants because they say yes to all of our demands. Nevertheless, it is up to you to develop your level of understanding and to make them **POSITIVE or NEGATIVE**. Your job is to **UNDERSTAND AND CLEAN UP**.

As humans, we have an emotional memory and have experienced negative, limiting emotions and positive, expansive emotions. A key point is to perceive whether we are emotionally addicted or not. We can express our freedom clearly when we are not trapped in the grip of fear, sadness or anger, emotions that we have all experienced. It is healthier, when such emotions appear not to hide or deny the accompanying feelings or to exaggerate them. As our understanding of this realm of the emotions develops, we begin to realise how it influences all areas of our life and this enables us to make freer choices of behaviour.

```
         BODY            MIND



      EMOTION         SPIRIT
```

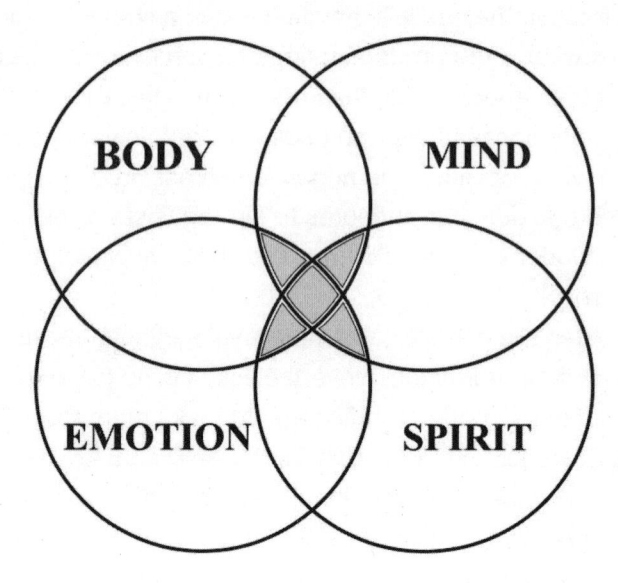

'...Guilt, anger, and fear hold us captive when the emotional body feeds off of fear. You can fake that you are not feeling anger, guilt, fear or sadness but there is no way around the emotion. Sooner or later, you will have to pass through it and absorb it with your consciousness. However, you can only absorb the emotions that you are aware of.' (Griscom, 1990)

In short, the key to moving forwards in all areas of your life is to integrate what you are and what your experiences of life have taught you.

'It is essential to integrate your divine identity through the vehicle of the emotions. This way, you come to understand the needs of that identity, its intuitive ability and what its source is and you can feel its energy and consciously work along with it. If not, your awareness will be endlessly subject to the realm of your emotions and these emotions will confuse your ability to see the truth, keeping you captive of your attitude of mind. This situation will feed on your energy, just like a possession does, keeping you trapped down at the same level on which it functions. Experiment with your emotional body for they are much more than just external forms of expression and experience. Being tied to the emotional body keeps you trapped at a physical level which keeps both your body and mind captive.' (Griscom, 1990)

From the programme: 'The Alchemy of Emotions'

The following exercise will help you discover thoughts and limiting belief patterns that underlie the results that you achieve in life. Emotionally speaking, be totally honest with yourself. Don't forget that they are just thoughts. Further on, you can read how to transform them, both for your benefit and for the benefit of others.

'The Personal Law' Questionnaire

1.- Five things that I like/d about my mother are...
2.- Five things that I don't/didn't like about my mother are...
3.- Five things that I like/d about my father are...
4.- Five things that I don't/didn't like about my father are...
5.- Five things that I like about my husband/wife/partner are...
6.- Five things that I don't like about my husband/wife/partner are
7.- Five things that I most like about myself are...
8.- Five things that I don't like about myself are...
9.- Something I wouldn't want other people to know about me is..
10.- Something I wouldn't want other people saying about me is
11.- Something I wouldn't want people thinking about me is...
12.- The biggest fear I have is…
13.- Something that I can't stand about myself is…
14.- The most negative thought I have about…

- Myself

- Life

- Men

- Women

- The family

- Love

- Money

- Friendship

- Work

- Sexuality

- Relationships

- Religion

15.- What does someone (anyone) have to believe/think/or feel about themselves to think/be/or do?

(questions 7, 9, 11 and from the first point of number 14 onwards until you reach a point of conclusion).

PERSONAL LAW: (The thought that comes up most or is repeated the most in the exercise or the one that you are most uncomfortable with).

ETERNAL LAW-The Affirmation: (Following is the explanation and how to use this marvellous tool).

Affirmations and the Eternal Law

You need to make the decision whether to free yourself from the bare rock that hides the wonderful sculpture of your essence or not. The human mind can be compared with a garden that is either wisely cultivated or left to its fate and abandoned. Both ways will bear fruit; if the seeds of useful plants are not planted and cultivated, then the seeds of less useful ones will eventually fall and germinate there to reproduce time and time again as weeds. To cultivate consciousness, to be able to grow, you need to **be aware of your Personal Law and replace it with a positive belief or affirmation that reconnects you with your fundamental nature and true essence.**

An affirmation is a consciously selected positive thought that is introduced into the mind via a process of repetition in order to achieve a new result that you want in your life. This means that you give your heart and mind the idea of a purpose. Your mind will come up with anything if you give it half the chance. The affirmation will help you sow the seeds of what you want to harvest and care for the plants that grow. Repetition (which is a natural process of the mind) helps you to feed your mind with positive thoughts about your goal and achieve what you desire. As believing is creating, everything that your mind focuses on will come true sooner or later. Remember that it is reason that serves the heart and the joy in your heart that serves your entire wellbeing.? With a positive and open mind, your heart becomes joyful and it is this joy that gives vitality to the body and makes life a celebration.

In Leonard Orr's book entitled 'Prosperity Consciousness Consultation', the father of Rebirthing writes that 'an affirmation is a statement of the unique life force flowing through each individual, an acceptance of each person's special gifts and opportunities. It is a positive life supporting statement chosen on purpose to replace former non-life supporting beliefs… Affirmations can help us to develop prosperity consciousness by redirecting our thoughts from habitual negative patterns to a fuller realisation of our true potential.'

So, if someone has a negative thought like 'I'm not good enough', they can replace this thought by thinking and writing the opposite thought, a version of which would be 'I, (name) am more than good enough. I love and accept myself. I am safe', or 'I (name) am highly pleasing to myself, especially in the presence of others'. The repeated use of an affirmation will progressively imprint it on your mind and simultaneously minimise and probably erase the old thought pattern, firmly bringing about the changes you wish to make in your life. A Course in Miracles says, 'All negative thought is an attack on God', and suggests carrying out the process of 'undoing and redoing'.

I am the thinker who thought I wasn't good enough. I am also the thinker who now thinks that I am perfectly good enough and I act accordingly.

In the same way that a gardener cultivates the earth by taking out the weeds and planting flowers and fruit trees, the human being can care for the garden of his or her mind by ridding it of all bad and useless limiting thoughts and by cultivating to perfection the flowers and fruits of correct and useful positive thinking.

The Characteristics of an Affirmation

- It will be in the first person.

- It will be in the present tense.

- Be specific and put your name in it.

- It will always be positive.

- It uses the key word (inability/ability; inadequate-adequate; don't deserve-deserve; dull-expressive; bad-good; ignorant-wise; useless-invaluable; guilt-innocence; need- abundance;

struggle-pleasure and ease; etc.).

- It will be meaningful to you so that you are encouraged to repeat it over and over again.

- It will have a sense of permanence (completeness, absoluteness, always, at any time, etc.)

Leonard Orr also suggests saying affirmations to yourself in the first, second and third persons because this is part of the language that we use and the way we communicate. He says that when we were in our mother's womb and when we were born, people referred to us in the third person by saying he or she. Later on, our parents and the teachers at school talk to us in the second person when they say you. Affirming the I, you and he/she is very powerful because it reaches down into the subconscious.

Dialogue: - What's the price of freedom?

- Your freedom in exchange for the mask? you hide behind, the mask that helps you to feel more comfortable. Yet it's difficult for you to discard it, not because it fits so well but because you've been wearing it for so long.

How to work with Affirmations

The best way to make affirmations is by writing them down so that they can become fulfilled ('action in the service of change'). Once you have your affirmation corresponding to the aforementioned characteristics, write it down on the left-hand side of a page in a notebook and use the right-hand side of the page (the 'emotional response column') to jot down any thought that the affirmation brings up or arouses in you. Repeat this many times (for example, write it out 20 times a day with a different response if possible every time you write the affirmation).

For example:

I (your name)	always express my feelings in the right way and at the right time	Not true
I (your name)	always express my feelings in the right way and at the right time	Lies!
I (your name)	always express my feelings in the right way and at the right time	That's scary!

Continue writing day by day until you start getting affirmative words and phrases appearing in the response column.

For example:

I (your name)	always express my feelings in the right way and at the right time	It's possible, I guess
I (your name)	always express my feelings in the right way and at the right time	I believe it.
I (your name)	always express my feelings in the right way and at the right time	IT'S TRUE!

Search for the problem of your false Self, which is what is creating the conflictual circumstances in your life and cut it at the roots to rescue your authentic Self which is suffering behind bars that prevent it from being free.

Success has to do with achievement and you can only be successful when your belief system supports the pursuit of your goals. As a human being, you have the privilege of being able to formulate new, attribute-orientated programmes for yourself that are aligned with your fundamental nature. You need to work on your belief system if you want to make important changes in order for your life to be more balanced. As Henry Thoreau said, 'A thousand notches inflicted on the leaves of the tree of evil is equivalent to just one on the root.' Your life will undergo a considerable improvement when you work on the main root-law of your belief system, which is where your outlook on life and behaviour originate. You will then begin to achieve results and become more fulfilled as a person.

If you haven't been able to glimpse what your root law is during the process of diagnosing and detecting your personal law, don't stop there for you can work with one of the branch laws that surround it. These will lead you sooner or later to the root law. You have more than one personal law, so the healing process around each law enables the process with the following one to flow more easily and to be more dynamic. It can also be really enjoyable. It's a bit like eating an artichoke where you peel off the leaves until you get to the heart, which is the tasty part and where the essence of the artichoke really is.

The intention of using affirmations is not to repress any negative thoughts that may come to you but to create a safe context in which you can recognise and feel these thoughts and then verbalise and change them. As Leonard Orr says, it's a matter of becoming more alert to the temptation of wishful thinking. 'Finding itself growing in a pear orchard, an apple tree might try repeating over and over, 'I am producing big, juicy, beautiful pears,' but it would only experience frustration.' The intention of the affirmation is to relax and be yourself. When you know who you are, your wealth extends way beyond your tremendous imagination. You are an unlimited being with infinite intelligence and the ability to manifest whatever you want.

Forgiveness

Forgiveness is another way of acting consciously to clear and change any thought, emotion or sensation that leaves you feeling alienated from your divine essence. Forgiveness sets you free because, by forgiving yourself and others, you give up the need to hide the guilt and shame that you feel as the result of having thought that you were a defenceless victim or that you have been relentlessly victimising others.

Why bother to forgive? When you forgive others you are loving yourself because you release your heart and mind from judgement and resentment. When you judge others, you only judge yourself and use the same yardstick for both yourself and them. Holding on to resentment means that you are keeping your memory and emotive nature busy with a painful memory and what the resentment does is to feed this and magnify it. Forgiveness turns the yardstick into a wand that sets you free and makes you generous with yourself, your surroundings and with others. By integrating experiences from the past and being free to celebrate the present moment, your memory and emotions can then offer themselves to serve you for a better life here and now.

Forgiveness is not suffering from amnesia but rather a freeing the heart and mind from judgement, grief and distrust. Forgiveness is loving and trusting by using experiences from the past as a support for your discernment of the present.

As with any process, it may seem that you don't have anything or know of anybody to forgive at the beginning. Your individual world, however, is a microcosm within the universal macrocosm where all energy exists. This means that all women represent your mother or your mother figure and you relate with the men in your life by copying the pattern that you established with your father or you father figure. You distinguish trust, help and sympathy according to the relationship that you have established with your faith, and the hands that you encounter in your life will have things in common with your obstetrician or midwife's hands. Forgive these five: yourself, your mother, your father, your religion and your obstetrician or midwife and you will clear your path of weeds, walls and chasms that are impeding your process of development.

Writing a forgiveness affirmation is done in the first person, just like other affirmations, and you can also include the second and third persons as well. Create the forgiveness affirmation with an open end and every time, you can finish the sentence off with an 'emotional response ending'.

For example:

I (your name) totally and lovingly forgive myself (I forgive my father / mother / religion / teacher) for ... not having respected myself (me).

I................totally and lovingly forgive myself (I forgive my father / mother / religion / teacher) for ... for having thought that I can't.

Forgiveness is a transformational process because it often starts as a task or treatment and turns into a conscious practice that is connected with love. When you start the work of Forgiveness, the ego will do everything in its power to divert your attention. Persist and remember that commitment and courage are two essential values in any form of transformation. You can start this process by writing the forgiveness affirmation from 35 to 70 times a day for seven days, beginning with one of the five that I mentioned above. Be mindful of the thoughts, feelings and emotions that come up when writing 'I forgive...' and just write down the emotional response without holding yourself back. That way you will get to know yourself better and know what to do and with greater effect.

You may need to repeat the process for some people and include others in the list (partner/husband/wife, mate, business partner, children, boss, brothers and sisters, friends, etc.).

Gratitude

Gratitude is a celebration of life. It is the acceptance of (or releasing the attachment to) every individual person, thing and incident that comes and goes at each moment of your life. It is acceptance of the path that life opens before you, whether you realise this or not, and even though it may at first appear to be contradictory, painful or ill-adjusted, you can be sure that it will serve as a stepping stone to progress. Gratitude is an act of humbleness before the magnificence of life. It is the acceptance of the moment in the instant that it occurs and being one with the flow of the momentum of life.

You can fortify your sense of gratitude with the following exercise. Every night, before your body totally relaxes in sleep, say to yourself: 'Something that I am especially grateful for today is...' and 'Something from the past that I am still especially grateful for today is...'; and every morning, before opening your eyes and in that initial moment on becoming lucid, say: 'I give thanks for today and all of the experiences, feelings and decisions that it brings me!'

With this intention of gratitude, your attitude of approval and recognition towards yourself and towards life becomes consolidated.

It is the acceptance and celebration of the essence of life.

The Potential of the Human Brain:

If you want to entirely transform your thoughts, you need to work with more of your brain's potential. This means using not only the reptilian brain and the limbic system but also the two hemispheres of the brain (the left side of the brain is associated with logic and science and the right side with imagination and art).

One can benefit the most from the two hemispheres of the brain through visualisation, and the key to visualisation is breathing.

Breathing

Breathing is an essential, biological act and it is synonymous with life. It is the first thing we do when we are born and the last thing we do before passing away. It is the source of all of our power in the physical world. It is something that is so automatic and obvious that we often go about our lives without realising that it is an active function in the body and that we depend on it to live. We are so unconscious of our breathing, however, that we don't realise how much our emotions affect it. When we are happy, we breathe fully, whereas a negative emotion can limit our breathing to such a degree that it causes the inhibition of all forms of holistic sustenance for us. Just think that most of the time, instead of breathing, we are merely sub-breathing or breathing just the minimum necessary to stay alive. It's like driving a powerful car in first gear all of the time. Of course, the bulk of our potential gets held back.

'Achieving mastery over breathing and thought is to achieve mastery over human consciousness.' (Orr et al, 1998)

This knowledge is as old as the history of man. The first breathing techniques were developed thousands of years ago and many cultures around the world are familiar with the use of breathing as a means of transformation. The start of a new holistic understanding and approach to the human psyche came at the end of the nineteen sixties when medicine and transpersonal psychology began to use breathing as a methodology for healing.

The brain is fed by oxygen, which has been absorbed into the blood flow that circulates through the lungs. Breathing exercises and disciplines increase this oxygen supply. The exercises, both in their ancestral and modern forms, are proven ways of accessing one's inner self for they are simple, safe and easy, and powerful at the same time.

Breathing consciously in a simple way is refreshing to the mind and body. Conscious breathing refreshes the vital energy in your body, it cleanses the nervous and circulatory systems, it nourishes your cells and internal organs of the body, and it cleanses and balances the body's aura.

Since early seventies, Leonard Orr has taught by way of his own example and through repetition: - 'Breathing is a practice and not just an awareness.'

Breathing is safe; living life to the full is safe!

Breathing in a conscious, connected way is like voyaging within the realm of being beyond words.

Visualisation

Visualisation is a powerful ally for maximising the human being's unlimited potential. The support elements are conscious breathing, key words, expressions (affirmation) and poetry, colour (including symbols and diagrams), flower essences, specific types of music and essential oils. A key word or expression is essential for activating the memory, while colours, flowers and essential oils enable one to be more creative and limitless (colours can be calming to the brain just like certain types of music). These elements awaken the holistic consciousness in the brain.

Thought works through repetition and it is for this reason that it is so powerful. You convey your mind and energy to whatever it is you are focusing on, you repeat it constantly on both the conscious and unconscious levels and you manifest it. **BELIEVING IS CREATING**. By imitating this same process and combining it with the key elements (conscious breathing, words, colour, flowers, essential oils and symbols and supported at times with a certain type of music), you visualise what you want and how to get it in a clear, simple and enjoyable way. What you achieve is a meaningful image that is easy to imagine and repeat that serves as the scale model in your mind that you need and can use immediately to start manifesting it in your normal, tangible reality.

The Holistic Collage

A holistic collage is similar to a photograph of the future created in the present. To make one, take a sheet of cardboard, some paper, colours markers, crayons and paintbrushes. From a selection of magazines, cut out images that portray how you would like to be. Find photographs, poetry and any other visual element that are inspiring to you. Fix these to the collage sheet to create a visual story.

Developing the collage is just like setting goals but in this case it is a goal that you set by using visual creativity. It should be a challenge for you and at the same time achievable and clear in its message. It should enable you to measure your progress, as every time you look at the holistic collage, it will activate your positive thinking, stimulated by the visualisation process. Every time you visualise what you want, the ideas expressed in the holistic collage develop and become closer to reality.

There are three key steps to making a successful holistic collage:

1 Give thanks instead of asking for what you desire. Write across the top of the collage: 'I (your name) am grateful for all of this'. This is a way of recognising that we are co-creators of our life.

2 After assembling your holistic collage and before signing, connect with your heart and mind and write at the bottom: 'This, or something better, manifests for me here and now, in harmony with everybody involved and the universe. Thank you' followed by your signature and date.

3 Prepare the holistic collage in a conscious and dedicated way, but be detached from your results. This way, you allow yourself the space to be able to give particular attention to the trust that you have in yourself and in the universe as a whole. You will learn about acceptance and how to handle the undertow of your longings. Imagine that you are an artist inspired with the work you have at hand. Experience and enjoy the whole process regardless of the

end result, connecting the conception of the idea to its development and completion and even beyond the finishing of the piece. Once a work of art is created, it generates a force and acquires a life of its own.

Be grateful, joyful and aware when making your holistic collage. Be efficient and determined to achieve your goal and accept your results. Remember: **you always get whatever you need for your higher evolution and development**.

Meditation, taking care of the seed that you have planted

Once you have the image firmly in your mind (the VISUALISATION) and materialised on paper (the HOLISTIC COLLAGE, a map to your treasure), it is also essential to 'care for the seed that you have planted so that it germinates and grows well' (affirmation or the eternal law). You need to create an appropriate space where you can learn to still the mind so that there is a pause between one thought and the next. This way, you can enhance the image of what you want (affirmation or the eternal law).

How can you achieve this? Wearing loose, comfortable clothing, choose a quiet place where you can sit in a chair with your feet firmly on the floor. If you prefer to sit on the floor, use a cushion so that you can fold your legs in such a way that they support your body. If necessary, put cushions under your knees as well. Whether you are sitting in a chair or on the floor, keep your back as straight as possible without it getting stiff. It is important to be as comfortable as possible. Put your hands on your thighs, close your eyes and focus on your breathing. Inhale deeply and evenly and breathe out slowly with every breath. You can also listen to music that you enjoy when doing this. Don't stay with your thoughts, observe them and let them pass by. Stay focused on your breathing and by using an affirmation. The time you spend meditating is not important. However, you will find that it progressively gets longer until the time you spend is appropriate for you.

By repeating the whole VISUALISATION process over and over again, positive thoughts gain ground in your mind and heart and begin to completely transform your negative thoughts.

A human being's potential is unlimited. It is merely a question of time, energy and space for it to expand.

'Our deepest fear is not of being inadequate. Our deepest fear is that we are powerful beyond our dreams. It is not the darkness that we are really frightened of but the light. You might ask how it is that we are all so brilliant, charming, talented and fabulous. When it comes down to it, why aren't we? We are all children of God. Our individual contribution, albeit small, is valid for everybody. There is nothing enlightening in withdrawing yourself from other people so they won't feel unsafe in your presence. We were born to manifest the glory of God that is inside of us, and not just some of us but all of us. As we let the light within us shine, we consciously allow others to do the same and when we rid ourselves of our fears, our presence automatically frees others.' (Williamson, 1992)

Transforming your limiting thoughts will transform the world and enable you to experience the celebration of life as a daily event.

I invite you to become aware of your negative thoughts and to acknowledge that they exist. Accept them and then act accordingly on them. In doing so, you will be able to consciously choose the future, for this is the process for bringing about real change: becoming aware of an aspect of yourself, accepting (approving of) it and acting accordingly.

The time that you take is not important; what is important is your commitment to your own process.

'The vision that you glorify in your mind, the ideal that you

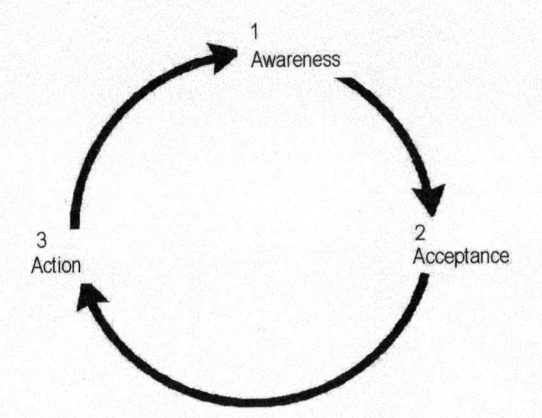

```
        1
    Awareness

3                2
Action       Acceptance
```

enthrone in your heart - this you will build your life by, and this you will become.' (Allen, 1903)

Life Circle Evaluation

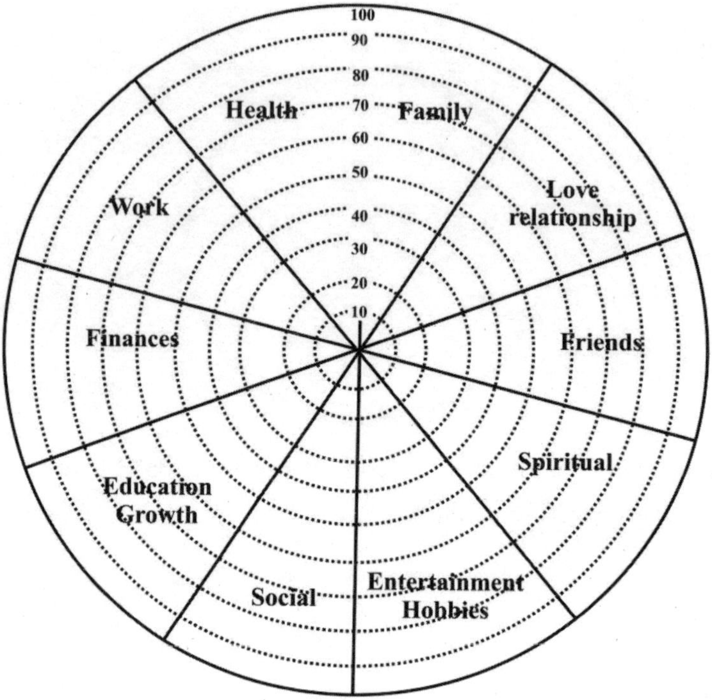
100
90
80
70
60
50
40
30
20
10
Health
Family
Love relationship
Friends
Spiritual
Entertainment Hobbies
Social
Education Growth
Finances
Work

Knowing where you are and how you're doing (the chapter that you have just read) and where you're going and how to get there (the chapter about vision) are fundamental characteristics of the leaders of today and the future. This is basic for being able to experience your freedom and to achieve a balanced shift in the different areas of your life, the whole of which is much greater than the sum of its parts.

To sum up

BEING	DOING	ACHIEVING	SUCCESS
Self-knowledge. The awareness and acceptance of one's being in a process of constant change	Accepting one's work as a mission and making use of the goodness in oneself and the universe as a gift and tool with which to evolve	Re-establishing contact with one's dreams, setting goals, carrying out plans of action that are in line with the planning and maintaining of an adaptable stance to change	Integrating values into your actions and integrating yourself with a conscious vision that is connected with everything in the universe: **(The Art and the Science of living).**

Satisfaction in life reaches its maximum expression when thought and action dance to the same rhythm.

Who Makes the Bed?

Chapter Five
The Transformation of Sexuality

Our sexuality is the most intimate, private aspect of who we are. It has to do with how we feel about being male or female. How comfortable are we really with our bodies, our sexual thoughts, our relationships and the expression of the feminine and masculine energies in our personalities?

The enticing pathway of developing our sexual consciousness expands the boundaries of relationships. We discover numerous strategies for opening up the dimensions of that joy, the flowing sensations of connection and ecstasy creating unity and completeness. Each partner develops their own personal feelings of harmony without losing themselves in the other as they transform their sexuality into an activity that is both positive and pleasurable. Sexual energy can bring a couple together into a dynamic tango of tenderness and passion, creating self-awareness and strengthening their self-esteem and commitment to one another.

The home base
The conscious sexual relationship becomes a nurturing home base for two equal beings where desires and needs are expressed on time, in a safe privacy, secure in the trust of the other. The emotional expression, the sweetness of this moment of intimacy brings with it a liberty, a freedom of choice, to lead or to follow in the dance. A bond of togetherness and complicity is built up during the adventure through the fun and laughter of the different sensual pleasures and positions. Beyond the physical sensations and the

emotions, there emerges an awareness of the value of the present moment, a shared consciousness that the privilege of travelling together on this journey is more precious than the climax of the orgasm.

Loving communication

The sexual act itself can certainly be physically satisfying, but in the absence of love it rarely brings a deep and lasting fulfilment of the spirit. The capacity to express love freely and openly, with joy and contentment, demands a self-confident use of our many skills of communication and the carefree ease of intimacy. Often, we will need to learn how to communicate more effectively to express that love in all its depth. Communication during healthy sex is caring and pleasurable, through the changing rhythms of the movement and breathing, through words and whispers, taste and touch, sight and sound. Consciousness of loving is the portal through which our sexuality transcends those fleeting moments of bliss into a colourful lasting nourishment of the soul.

Healthy or toxic sex

Sexual desire is a powerful force in the human mind, helping us to develop as sexual beings. Its capacity to lead us into a greater consciousness in our loving relationships is boundless. However, like most powerful forces, it can be channelled into either healthy or toxic experiences. The toxic side of desire is capable of leading us into a number of destructive and addictive behaviours. The betrayals of authority that include incest and child abuse are driven by misdirected sexual desire and in violent acts like rape and assault. Such toxic energy can shatter trust and destroy a person's sense of self-worth and safety.

Alone or together

You don't need to be in a relationship to develop a healthy sexuality;

many exercises of development also work well for singles, such as self-touch, massage and spending time naked. For example, exploring your body with a mirror will help you to improve your appreciation of all your body, the areas you like and those you like less.

However, if you do have a partner, you both need to become educated about the sexual learning strategies for participating actively and effectively in the process. If your partner doesn't want to join you at first, because of denial or shame, blaming you or conditioning taboos, you could start working on this by yourself. The effects of the transformations in your own behaviour can serve to attract your partner toward the process.

Where do you stand
Situating where you are today with your personal attitudes is an important first step in the process of developing a deeper consciousness of the subject. Where do your beliefs and behaviours locate you in the overall picture of sexuality? If you have any doubts about the nature of your sexuality, check the following comparisons chart by Wendy Maltz which highlights the contrasts between the beliefs that lead towards Sexual Addiction and Abuse and those that will help to develop Healthy Sex.

Comparisons chart

Addiction and Sexual Abuse	Healthy Sex
Sex is uncontrollable energy	Sex is controllable energy
Sex is an obligation	Sex is a choice
Sex is addictive	Sex is a natural drive
Sex is hurtful	Sex is nurturing, healing
Sex is devoid of love	Sex is an expression of love
Sex is 'doing to' someone	Sex is sharing pleasure with someone
Sex is void of communication	Sex requires communication
Sex is secretive	Sex is private
Sex is exploitative	Sex is respectful
Sex is deceitful	Sex is honest
Sex benefits one person	Sex is mutual
Sex is emotionally distant	Sex is intimate
Sex is irresponsible	Sex is responsible
Sex is risky and unsafe	Sex is safe
Sex has no limits	Sex has boundaries
Sex is power over someone	Sex is empowering
Sex requires a double life	Sex enhances who you really are
Sex compromises your values	Sex reflects your values
Sex feels shameful	Sex enhances self esteem

How you think about sex significantly affects how you and your partner will experience and feel about it. Pick up on any of the contrasting assertions that concern or trouble you. You may want to discuss these with a friend, a wise person in your family, a mentor, a counsellor or a health educator, to understand the differences more.

Evolution of sexuality through the years
No matter where we find ourselves on the journey of our sexuality, whether sexual activity has disappeared from our relationship or is present and balanced, or has spiralled down into addictive or compulsive behaviour, we can all benefit from improving the connection.

Our sexual energy will not have a constant level through the years. It does not have a static quality. Both males and females will experience a range of differing libido levels during their lifespan. From the age of puberty, through sexual maturity to the eldest of ages, we live the awakening experiences of menstruation, erections, and spontaneous ejaculations. We discover masturbation and orgasm, we traverse pregnancy, breast-feeding and menopause, we can suffer sexual dysfunctions due to stress and illnesses and we can be afflicted by ovarian cysts or prostate complications amongst others.

Dance with the changes
The journey is long, but one thing is clear. When our sexuality is healthy, we will be able to dance with the changes that life's processes will bring us instead of sliding into depression, denial and indifference. The sexual energy that we give and receive within our relationship does not depend uniquely on intercourse. There is a whole range of intimate loving and sensual expression to be shared through touch, massage, tenderness and caring communication. This is an intimacy that really nourishes our souls and bodies.

Wide Horizons

This day of Eros on the island of Aphrodite
I feel you reach out with love,
Your faith finds me empty but open,
Freed of the clinging fog of confusion.
Love's rush, warm and tender,
Enfolds me in its generous embrace,
Tingling up my spine, pouring my heart full.
I drink of you, quenching this thirst,
Held to your breast by woman's arms,
Touched to tears by the gift of your dreams.
A meeting of lovers, a Latin surprise,
A waiting ended, uncertainty dissolved.
Still trembling with emotion, my commitment grows,
Borne by love-song, released across foaming blue ocean,
Soaring joyful, sobbing and laughing,
Winging past cloudless desert and orange parched sand
Starbursting silver onto tropical shores.
Helios reclaims the skies above,
My life set out before me with wide horizons,
The teachings laden with delight, whispering love's invitation
Like a fig tree in full fruit.

Chapter Six
Daring to be Sexually Healthy

The sexual relationship provides one of the deepest channels for the expression of love and appreciation. Regular demonstrations of approval and tenderness between partners builds trust in the constancy of love, the durability of the relationship and the safety of intimacy. We are deeply nourished by the love and appreciation that we receive from our partner simply for being who we are. This is why it is so important for us to be able to express easily, in return, our own love and appreciation for our partner. This depth of mutual trust in the intimate relationship is created gradually, progressively, through a continuity of positive experiences of a partner's dependability. Trust develops a couple's capability to resolve, side by side, the trials that life will inevitably bring to the relationship. Trust is something that is earned, it has to be deserved, to be merited and, in return, the self-confidence generated by the feelings of being trusted by your partner is, like an award, a wonderful gift to receive.

Daring to be vulnerable
When you feel trusting and trusted and in safety with your partner, the feelings of security and intimacy make it possible to really open yourself up to them with your defences lowered, vulnerable and fully present withholding nothing. Expressing your deepest longings, talking about and even releasing, the fears and shames that you may have been secretly shouldering for years. We often conceal these self-doubts and shameful feelings because we fear that our

partner's knowledge of our weaknesses will diminish their love for us. But this self-created shield of protection, unfortunately, will also mask and cloud over many of our deepest qualities. We will actually be camouflaging our true selves, our core vibration, from our beloved partner. This gap, created by our fear of being too deeply known, will stand between us and diminish our ability to get really close to them, into that intimate spot of bliss, that safe place by their side where we can feel the strength of the security created by our relationship. Daring to be vulnerable is no small achievement. Intimacy without showing our vulnerability is not possible.

The key to sexual intimacy

To allow vulnerability to appear, we have to overcome our fears and face up to the risks of losing our loved one, plunging ourselves into the pain of separation and loneliness. Exploring those dreads, feeling the fear and releasing it from deep within yourself will reveal the courage you require to become vulnerable. After all, if your partner fails to appreciate you for whom you really are, maybe it is time to be moving on. The paradox is that by giving yourself permission to become vulnerable, accepting to remove your body armour, throwing open the windows of your heart and revealing your precious soul to the steady gaze of the loved one, are all key actions to creating profound sexual intimacy. Nobody can know the healing flow of that intimacy until they have known vulnerability.

'In true intimacy, the other one is our inspiration'. Michael Gurian.

Our delicate nakedness

Our capacity to go into deep intimacy with a partner will have a strong influence on how we live our sexuality in the relationship. Our physical surrender to the other, our creative and spontaneous expressions of joy and pleasure and the carefree movements that characterise healthy sexuality, will all find their place in that intimate atmosphere. We entrust our partner with the freedom and knowledge of our most private spaces and truths, knowing that they will respect the delicate nakedness of our body and mind. Secrets no longer find a place to hide. With the courage to develop intimacy, we can ride 'the unbearable lightness of being' that characterises conscious loving relationship.

Basic urges
Healthy sexuality is a rich development taking us far beyond our instinctive geniality. Driven by the hormones of physiological need, simple geniality satisfies the primary urges stirred up in the context of a 'one-night stand'. In such encounters, the sexual relation has its initiation and its culmination in the bed and though the sexual excitement can be hot and physically satisfying, the time spent together is usually limited and the genital satisfaction will not last long. Later, there will remain little depth to the partner's knowledge of each other beyond the recognition of the strong and mutual basic urges that brought them together.

Between the sheets
However, for the partners who have decided to build a conscious and loving sexual relationship, what happens between the sheets, at a chosen moment, is not the beginning of that particular sexual connection, but actually the culmination of a whole series of meaningful contacts that the partners have shared during the day, connected by their complicity with one another in a mutual pampering. They have been walking together throughout the day on a soft, erotic, underlay which has cleared their hearts and fired their spirits, releasing their bodies to share and enjoy their sexuality.

Who makes the bed
A couple gets together with the day's tasks completed or not, but holding no resentments or secrets in their hearts, because their day's conflicts and misunderstandings have been resolved with care

and then let go of. Their day has in fact been a journey lived with awareness of the loving, intimate simplicity of its shared moments. Activities such as a pre-breakfast walk in the rising sun, the laughter about who makes the bed, the joint choice of her day's earrings, the lunchtime conversation about the complications that have come up for him at work and the actions needed to help heal a child's illness have touched them both. Contemplations of the evening beauty of the sea and the sky, sharing during the cooking together in the kitchen, incidents remembered together, of the excitements of first loves, accounts of dreams dreamed in each other's embrace, talking over ideas and feelings and accepting differing points of view, and all this amongst a scattering of tender passing glances, touches and smiles, intimately exchanged here and there among the routine duties of the day. Even if this couple may not have the time intentionally set aside for making love or creating the comfortable and intimate surroundings that they most enjoy, they are openly sexually available to each other, relaxed and full of affection and desire.

Blocking sexual energy
Could another couple, in crisis, with emptiness in their communication, eaten dry by the bitterness of unresolved conflicts, harried by persistent criticism and disrespect, harbouring mutual feelings of chronic mistrust and without shared horizons in front of them, could such a couple have any motivation whatsoever to agree on generating the erotic charge which would allow them to move together towards a loving sexual encounter? Inspired by Sergio Sinay's, "Healing the couple".

The essential components
In a conscious relationship, healthy sexuality, intimacy and elements of erotism are essential components of each day, alongside love, communication, trust and commitment, where the shared journey is

nourishing and self-sustaining. Situating where you are today with your personal attitudes about sexuality is an important step in the process of developing a deeper consciousness of the subject.

Daring to do these 7 steps

1-Effective communication
2-Frequent expressions and demonstration of love
3-Healthy sexuality
4-Intimacy and eroticism elements
5-Trust and commitment
6-Accepting and respecting the differences
7-Continuous learning and sense of humour

The Colour of my love.

Time lingers over my working hours
Running jerkily onward, focus fuzzy, sound confused
An atmosphere creeping upon me stark and lean
While wood burns to ashes in the stove
The emptiness in this house without your heat
Leaves me reaching for boundaries not there
Soft arms which cannot hold me
Brown eyes which do not see me
When I dare to look for them
Symptoms of your absence take such lonely forms.

The moment love tunes my heart with yours
Colour surrounds me in this rich home
Love sings me the song of our relationship
Words through two arches, food round a table
Juice across a garden, passion on silky sheets
Minds and bodies intertwined belly on belly,
Heart to heart, breath in breath
Empty of thoughts, our circle of wonder
New every day.
This is my love for you.

Chapter Seven
The Healing Process of Shared Vision

What draws a couple closer to each other, or pushes them further apart, is their everyday behaviour, the way that they choose, or manage, to relate to each other during the many moments of connection that fill their lives. This behaviour is closely tied to values and principles and the behaviour of each partner will reflect what is held in their core which, in turn, influences their vision of life, be it conscious or unconscious. These components are all related, none are isolated or stand alone.

In order to a create a shared vision it is important to develop each partner's individual vision. Following the detailed exercises from my book "Breathing the Rhythm of Success" (1999) you can articulate your own life purpose and vision. Once this individual work is completed, then you and your partner can share your results. You can then take the common elements from each, add some more value to it and co-create your vision as a couple. It is simpler when you follow the exercise step by step.

Life Purpose and Vision

A hologram can be described as the whole of something that can be projected in its entirety from just one part. Your life as a whole, on a day-to-day basis, is made up of your feelings, thoughts, the things you imagine and dream, your relationships with others, your sense of meaning of life, your daily living activities, and what you do and go about achieving.

Assume your purpose in life is to live in a continuous healing process for your imagination and your wisdom. A healing process in your relationship with yourself and others, in your sense of service and your achievements.

The ability to dream is one of the most powerful natural human talents we have been gifted with. Dreaming and taking action so that your heart's desire comes true is one of the most powerful decisions that you can make. 'The world belongs to those who dream,' or so the saying goes. Of course, we have all had a great dream of doing something at some point in our lives, but why do some people achieve their dream while others don't? Why do some people succeed while others don't? The answer, quite simply, is that you have to act upon your heart's desires. What does that mean? It means making an IDEAL REAL.

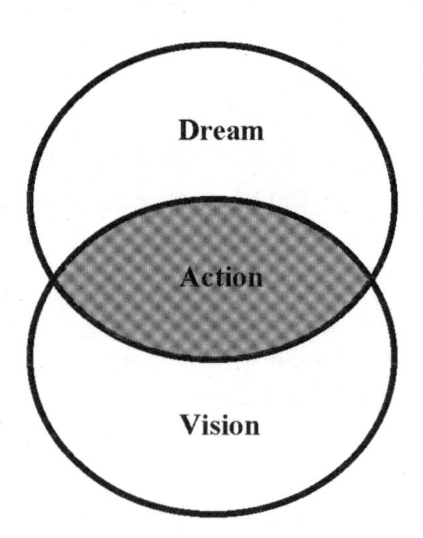

Dream

Action

Vision

So how can you act upon your heart's desires? How can you work on making your dreams come true whilst your interpretation of tangible reality is limiting what you are dreaming of?

Talking of the future, there are three types of people: those who let things occur, those who make them occur and those who ask themselves what happened.

You have to decide which group you belong to and then accept the responsibility for your decision. Each of the aforementioned three types of people obtains results, and these results depend on your decision, on how you see the world and how you participate in it.

Explaining why you made the decision that you did is a matter of being emotionally honest enough to be able to identify your excuses and also, of working on yourself and on external factors to transform the excuses. One of the most common excuses is everyday chores. Everyday chores never prevented anyone from following their heart's desire. They may slow you down in the fulfilment of your vision but they don't necessarily have to impede you. They can even stimulate you. *There is only one thing that makes a dream impossible and that is the fear of failure.*

The world is in the hands of those who have the courage to dream and run the risk of living according to their heart's desire.

The human being is in constant movement and this is the fundamental reason why different civilisations have developed since the remote times of primitive man. By challenging his fear of the unknown, humankind has opened new routes over land and sea in order to materialise their infinite dreams.

The Inner Urge

Self-knowledge is a good place to start any process of personal development, whether it is at the individual, family, social or business level, for it helps you to increase your level of awareness and to recognise your situation at the present time. As you become progressively more aware of your current situation and understand how you behaved at different moments in your life and why, it becomes easier for you to recognise and accept this. By accepting (approving of) it, you can make decisions and act on them.

Most of the time we dread the thought of starting a process to

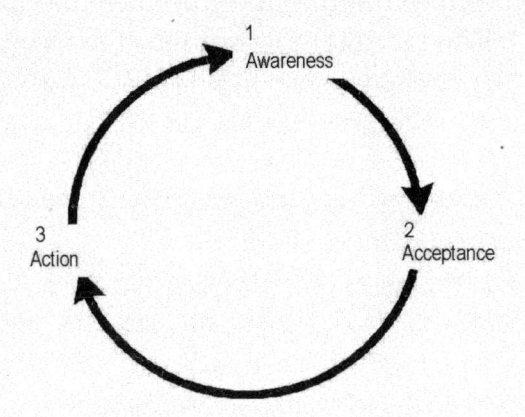

```
        1
    Awareness
   ↗          ↘
  3            2
Action      Acceptance
   ↖          ↙
```

find out what is really going on inside of ourselves. What comes to mind first is either the things that you haven't achieved or the suspicion that you will find out about something that you don't like. Beyond these fears of whatever you might have done or dread, however, there is a great treasure chest that contains the **NATURAL GIFTS belonging to mankind. Each one of us has natural gifts and specific attributes that are in harmony with our purpose in life.**

'...Everyone has a purpose in life... a unique natural gift or special attribute to offer to others. As we blend this attribute with service to ourselves and others, we experience the ecstasy and exultation of our spirit...' (Chopra, 1992)

It is of utmost importance to use the natural gifts that are part of our essence as human beings. It is up to us and how clear we are whether they work for us or against us. Our task is to discover them and to get them to work for us according to a system of principles and values so that they have a favourable impact on us and our surroundings.

Having a favourable impact on our surroundings has to do with expanding our consciousness. Accepting your skills and using them to grow will contribute to awareness and overall result.

According to the theory of morphic resonance, different species can learn, develop and adapt according to a process of parallel expansion. A discovery or achievement can contribute to a similar or much greater one at the same time in any other part of the world without there being any type of material communication between the two. Such stages of creation are directed by so-called morphic resonance, which explains what quantum physics describes in parallel worlds.

Each time we make use of our skills to grow, the light within us becomes bright and expands, which in turn leads to another light shining bright; like a centrifugal force, each achievement supports and energises all of the others, with events occurring simultaneously.

'...The source of all creation is pure consciousness... pure potentiality seeking expression from what is non-manifested to the manifested. And when we realise that our true self is pure potentiality, we align ourselves with the power that manifests everything in the future.' (Chopra, 1992)

This is where we become influential in the circles in which we move, whether it be the family, at work or socially. Influential leaders are people with a vision of their future, their passion motivating them to turn it into a reality and thoroughly enjoying themselves as they live out their dreams. They are people who know that they cannot stop dreaming because their heart's desire is what nourishes their soul, just as food nourishes their bodies. An influential leader is someone who, by means of his or her natural gifts, has achieved private victories that harmoniously drive them forward towards global victory.

Your Inner Urge and Driving Force United as One

'Man's duty is to dream and to pursue his heart's desire. When he wants something, the whole universe conspires to make his wish come true.' (Coelho, 1993)

Your inner urge gives you clarity concerning yourself, as well as the vision you have of what you want and your resulting actions, but that vision is made real and you truly live it when your inner urge joins together with the driving force of the universe that conspires with you.

The possibility of making a dream come true is precisely what makes life interesting. Dr. Victor Frankl wrote in his book 'Man's search for meaning', 'it is a special characteristic of man that he is able to project himself into the future. This is his salvation, even in the most difficult moments of his existence'.

When you have a dream that appears to be unattainable, you have three choices:

1.- Make it attainable by making a plan that includes action.

2.- Put it to one side.

3.- Struggle to achieve it without doing any prior planning.

How can you stay focused on the vision that you have of the future and not put it to one side?

The fear of suffering is worse than suffering itself and no-one's heart has really been afflicted while they have been pursuing their heart's desire. 'When you give up your dreams you experience an apparent peace and tranquillity that last briefly. However, your dreams that have died start to rot inside of you and they contaminate the air where you live, leaving the 'fight' (or the disappointment and defeat) that you tried all along to avoid as the sole legacy of your cowardliness.' (Coelho, 1993)

How can you avoid having to struggle so much to achieve your dream of something?

'Whoever you are and whatever you do, if you wish for something strongly enough it is because the desire had its origin in the spirit of the universe beforehand …and it is your mission here on Earth.' (Coelho, 1993)

There is no merit in aimless action, for it can easily turn into struggle. Taking action without a strategy will not make you a hero in life. All it will do is to merely add you to the group of people that do, do, do but with a persistent sense of futility. This just increases your feelings of impotence and victimisation.

'The heights by great men reached and kept were not attained by sudden flight, but they while their companions slept, were toiling upward in the night'.[6]

Fear is what makes one cling to the little that one has. It is said that there are two ways that you can be lost; by not knowing where you are and by not knowing where you are going. The more you get to know yourself, the more you start letting go of the fear of failure and being released from this fear will leave you free to choose where you want to be, now and in the future.

There is no error in the virtue that communicates with the power of creation. Insofar as you give out of virtue and are totally conscious of being and doing, there is no error. Error arises in the limited mind that thinks that doing is just an individual impulse instead of being one with the awareness of everything.

Whatever my dream is, it will be just perfect for me. I possess the power and ability to transform anything for I have natural gifts and virtues that work to my benefit and I am the holder of the power of thought. I am the creator of my thoughts and I can transform them to achieve any result I wish. I am clear in myself and I now give myself permission to dream.

When you were a child or adolescent, you were probably reprimanded for dreaming. This is why specialists say, 'You shouldn't limit a child's ability to dream'. It doesn't matter if the child says he wants to be a policeman one day, a fireman the next and a teacher the day after that. Encourage your child to dream for this will serve as his (or her) foundation in life. It could be possible for him to be a fireman, a policeman and a teacher all at the same time in an activity that enables him to serve others, which is really what he is putting across with his little heart's desire.

In his book on Future Vision, Joel Barker tells the story of a writer who, early one morning, meets a boy on the beach joyfully and carefully collecting starfish left stranded by the low tide. The writer reacted by saying: 'Young man, do you believe that what you are doing is worthwhile, there's thousands of miles and thousands of starfish...?' to which the boy responded by showing him the starfish that he had in his hand and was about to throw back into the sea 'It's worth it for this starfish...'. It took the writer a few hours to understand the boy. The next day, he went down to the beach and, together with the boy, began throwing starfish back into the water, knowing that although they could not collect them all, at least they could save quite a lot of them. In other words, he became part of the process instead of just remaining an observer of it.

If the writer had not listened to the boy who was throwing starfish back into the sea to save them, and if he had not thought about it, he could not have collaborated with him on throwing the starfish back into the sea. So, what do you do? Do you end up doing nothing where you are, living from one day to the next without knowing why? Of course not, you can choose to take part in the process. Each of us has something to offer in our own way. Simone De Beauvoir said that, 'The present is not the past in the making, the present is the moment of choice and action.'

Now is the time to choose and to take action. It is important to know where you are, where you are headed and what you can change in your world. By sharing external events instead of resisting them, you will find yourself taking control of your life. The sea isn't always calm and storms sometimes set in but it will become easier for you to understand them and to weather them out. It's not that nothing is ever going to happen. Things have happened and they will continue to happen. However, it is you that will change in your attitude to external events.

Don't resign yourself to saying that life is like that. Look for alternatives. Remember that you are a seeker.

As one awakens, fear and criticism give way to contemplation and virtue.

By using your ingenuity together with your actions, you can become the perfect strategist of your own life.

The Self joyfully and lovingly experiences Rebirth by taking responsibility for fulfilling what it does with its heart, mind and hands.

Your Natural Gifts

You have to start with something and what is yours are the multitude of **NATURAL GIFTS** and virtues that all of us humans possess. In each of us, one particular group of these gifts will stand out, making us unique and different from each other. Each one of us can put these natural gifts to work, serving both ourselves and others, so that we can plan a strategy and create a vision of the future that we deserve.

Imagination is one natural gift that we all have. It could also be stated that events and things are in the minds of people before they are actually created. By using my imagination, I can first create a 'model' and then a full scale 'building'. This applies to both tangible and intangible things.

This is to say that we carry out the action of creating before we actually receive anything. We are not usually aware of our power to 'believe, create and achieve' in our daily lives. We sometimes create in a positive way and at other times in a negative way. As our recognition and awareness of this natural positive power within us develops, we can direct it outwards to achieve what we deserve.

Cultivating virtues is like cultivating flowers. They grow slowly and as each one fills out, they are able to develop other virtuous characteristics until finally, the criticism and fear that were originally present become transformed by the alchemical process into elements that create virtue and they then gently blend together.

We are capable of changing the world by putting our vision of the future into practice. By recognising our natural gifts and virtues, putting them into practice and cultivating them, we offer what we are and what we do to the service of both ourselves and others.

Joel Barker, in his work on vision, says that, 'a dream without action is merely a dream, while action without vision of the future doesn't make any sense. Putting a vision of the future into practice, however, can change the world'. This is a good motto.

If my natural gifts and virtues make me different from other living beings and give me strong support in making my dreams come true, how can I 'rediscover' them?

The following exercise will help you to prepare your **VISION** and then to pinpoint your **PURPOSE IN LIFE**. You can start by choosing the internal and external characteristics of yourself that you like the most. These are your main **NATURAL GIFTS** and **VIRTUES** (e.g. being supportive, being responsible, my spirituality, my eternal quest to be a better person, my organising ability, my intuition, being a mother, being a father, my eyes, my smile, my get-up-and-go, etc.).

Be careful not to focus on your weaknesses at the cost of your natural positive gifts, as this would be detrimental to many areas of your life. Negativity affects your self-esteem and physical wellbeing and leaves you feeling powerless, creating a feeling of 'struggle' that will burden you down. Neither healthy nor constructive criticisms are useful here because criticism comes from judgement and judgement comes from condemnation and disapproval. Criticism, coming from oneself or others, restricts both the artist and scientist that we all carry inside of us. Feedback instead, as the word implies, feeds back into our self-observance, our inquisitive analysis and the possibility of improvement.

Our duty is to transform criticism and struggle and transcend from a mere level of survival to living a pleasant and fulfilling life, where we can contribute everything that we have to give to the world. If we focus on our positive characteristics, they will be our strengths. By recognising our strengths and attributes, they become our allies and support for transforming our weaknesses. **When somebody goes through an evolutionary process, everything around that person also evolves. 'When we strive to become better than we are, everything around us becomes better, too.'** (Coelho, 1993)

EXERCISE

Part I:

The 21 characteristics that you most like about yourself are:

My.....................   My.....................

My.....................   My.....................

My.....................   My.....................

My.....................   My.....................

My.....................   My.....................

My.....................   My.....................

My.....................   My.....................

My.....................   My.....................

My.....................   My.....................

My.....................   My.....................

My.....................

Part II:

Choose the 5 characteristics that you most like about yourself (out of the 21, part 1).

My.....................   My.....................

My.....................   My.....................

My.....................

The Healing Process of Shared Vision

Part III:

Write down 3 ways of expressing each of your chosen characteristics or natural gifts to the world (by creating or doing what and how) for your benefit and that of others.

a..........................

b..........................

c..........................

a..........................

b..........................

c..........................

a..........................

b..........................

c..........................

a..........................

b..........................

c..........................

a..........................

b..........................

c..........................

Part IV:

Choose the 5 ways of expressing yourself that you like the most. The order is not important.

1. ....
2. ....
3. ....
4. ....
5. ....

Part V:

The 21 things you most enjoy doing are: Example: dancing, eating, travelling, learning, reading, etc.

1- ....
2- ....
3- ....
4- ....
5- ....
6- ....
7- ....
8- ....
9- ....
10- ....
11- ....
12- ....
13- ....
14- ....
15- ....
16- ....
17- ....
18- ....
19- ....
20- ....
21- ....

Part VI:

Select the 5 things you most like doing (from the 21, part V).

1-...................... 4-......................

2-...................... 5-......................

3-......................

The next part of the exercise is about writing your Vision of the Future. Bear in mind the following:

Hints for creating your Vision:

Always start with your most expansive vision instead of ending with it. Don't set yourself small goals if your vision is far-reaching. Your dream must be large-as-life, a vision for yourself that you use to transform your present reality. If not, you run the risk of underestimating what you need and limiting yourself, of doing things without any sense of direction or even of doing something that isn't aligned with your vision of the future. This doesn't make sense and is also a waste of the precious energy that you need to create and produce what you want.

The action starts by stating your dream in writing. The first step is to transfer the idea of your dream or goal onto paper. It doesn't matter if your dream right now is to become a pilot; there are numerous ways that this can be interpreted (maybe part of your dream is about flying, being in a plane, moving from one place to another, or from one city to another). Further on, we'll see what your true wishes really are.

Don't let the way that you see the present situation limit your vision. The description of your dream is for yourself only and you don't have to share it with anyone if you don't want to. Nobody can steal your dreams because your thoughts and imagination are yours. What you are doing here is simply using your dreams to guide you to the actions required to materialise the dream life. Talk about it, write it down and follow the action plan.

Let the leader in YOU formulate your vision. You lead your own life, so it is only you who can create your personal vision of the future. From there, you can then go on to your vision for your family, business and friends or whatever. Once you have completed your own personal vision, share it with your family or partner because two or more have greater power to make something come true. Those who are running a business, for example, should make the vision for the company and share it with all of the personnel.

Take your life as a whole into account. This includes your personal life (mind, body, emotions and spirit), your family, work, social life and the world.

Express it in the present tense. It is better to express your vision in the present tense rather than letting it be conditioned by the future. Your vision is a photograph taken in present time of what you want in the future.

Your vision should be positive and encouraging. Focus on what is positive and not what is negative. Thought can be focused either way but the resulting energy is totally different from one to the other. Referring to the years he spent as a prisoner in a concentration camp, Dr. Victor Frankl says that his goal in any situation that he found himself in was to survive, to see how he could help others and to learn. Having something highly important to do in the future is what keeps us going in life and gives it meaning. Projecting ahead into the future is man's salvation and your vision should substantiate such an endeavour.

It should be detailed and comprehensive. It is important to know why, how, where, when and with whom.

Focus on yourself without manipulating others. When referring to family relations and close friends, visualise yourself with them in such a way that respects their individuality and independence.

It's better to aim too high than too low. Don't let your current situation or the ways that you interpret it limit you in any way. Once you have declared your vision and outlined your mission, you can go on to working on the near future by way of short term objectives and your corresponding plan of action.

Your natural gifts are tools that you can always rely on to make progress and advance in life and things will come easily to you if you use them. In my case, what I most like about myself is my intuition, my way with words, my dedication to serve, my eyes, how I support others and my enterprising nature. Even before I found out about all of this, these tools were the most efficient things that I had whenever I was in difficulties as well as being my most trusty and efficient companions when creating anything past and present.

Take account of what you most enjoy doing. Your dream is about having fun so include at least 5 of your favourite pleasures.

Mention the place where you live and the state of the world in general. Visualise the place or city and country where you live and what they are like. Always focus on what is positive. Include a description of what the world as a whole is like in your dream.

Include something altruistic. This is one of the factors that will make your vision truly far-reaching. For example, if you could give just an hour of your time every year to provide some altruistic service to others, whereabouts in the world and how would you dedicate this time (for example, taking care of abandoned children, the elderly and homeless, ex-alcoholics, turtles on the verge of extinction, dolphins, trees, rivers, etc.)? Include this in your dream so that you form part of everything; 'I am part of this planet. It matters to me and I care for it'. If you are willing to give more, that's fine, but if each one of us gave just this small amount, the planet would be a much better place to live. This intent really exists inside all of us; it's just that sometimes we can't find the way to channel it. This, on the other hand, is an excellent way. Just set yourself one simple and easy thing. Remember: the easier those things are, the easier it will be for you to achieve them.

Values and principles. Make sure that your vision is grounded in values and principles either by implying them or by making specific reference to them. This way, they affirm the integrity of your vision.

It's OK to define your vision and then change it later. The description of your vision is 'not going to be carved out of marble' so you can revise and adapt it if you want.

To sum up:
Your vision of the future should be encouraging, positive and

written in the present tense. Take your mind, body, emotions and spirit into account as well as your social life (you aren't isolated from the rest of the world). Mention the person/people who you are living with and those who you have contact with. Your vision is about you and the world around you. Describe where you live and the state of the world. Include your values and principles and mention your altruistic service to others. Make sure that you include what you most enjoy doing, together with your natural gifts for they will be your greatest allies.

Part VII:

See yourself at some point between 4 and 8 years in the future. Write down how you would like to see yourself, where you would be, what you would be doing and with whom, the conditions and so forth. Refer to the section on the 'Features to include in your Vision'. **My vision for the future is... -**

Part VIII:

Using your natural gifts and what you most enjoy doing, take this opportunity to outline your PURPOSE IN LIFE. Simple and yet very profound (as can be seen from the diagram), the process of doing this is a delight.

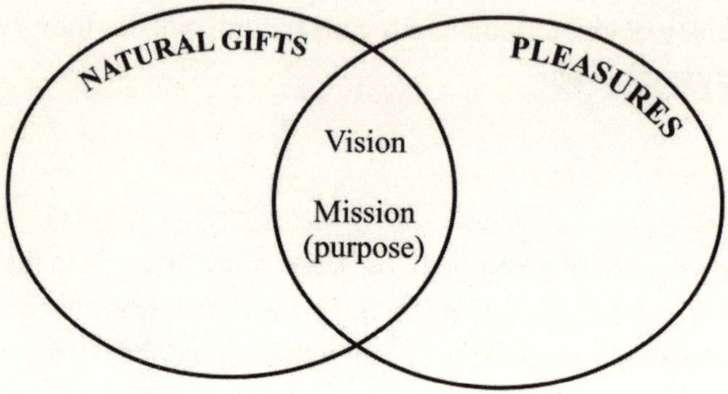
NATURAL GIFTS
PLEASURES
Vision
Mission
(purpose)

From the beauty and profoundness of what you have just discovered, write this sentence out and add the parts as suggested below:

My purpose in life is to use my... (Part II of the exercise) to... (Part IV) and thereby live... (Part VII).

The Holistic Nature of Humankind

Humankind is what connects heaven and earth. Both are part of him, united in his essence that is endowed with the natural gifts, virtues and attributes that make this connection possible.

The divine: The most divine aspect of the human being is our infinite ability to dream and imagine. We look to the heavens to dream, for it is there that we connect with the infinite. Your Vision of the Future belongs here for it is a long-term achievement.

The essence: Your essence is the love and passion to live life and other natural gifts that you treasure in your heart and that make what is divine possible. Even though man may pretend to run after wisdom, money and power, his life on the face of the Earth can be summarised as a search for love. Your mission or purpose in life also forms part of this essence, the medium term in time between two dates established by Heaven and Earth in what is really the eternal, for your essence is always there to accompany you.

Being grounded: Due to the marvel that distinguishes us from other living beings, we are capable of seeing far and near and of using our energy to project ourselves through time and space with the power of the mind and spirit in contact with the energy of the universe. It is very important to stay grounded and to know what one can depend on or not in order to achieve goals that are in tune with our heart's desire. The ability to define and state goals and plans of action for this purpose forms part of being grounded. In terms of time, we are talking about the short term.

This chapter forms part of the programme 'Alchemy of the Emotions'.

What distinguishes the holistic nature of one person from that of another is the balance between these three aspects, the divine, one's essence and the degree to which one is grounded.

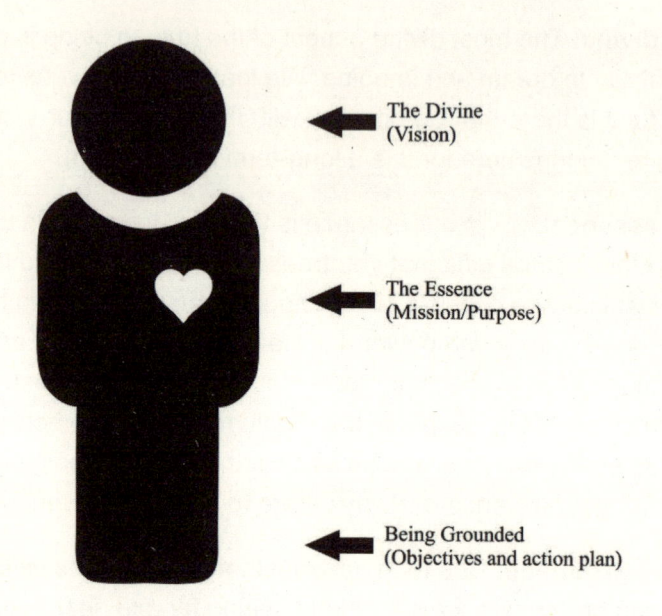

← The Divine (Vision)

← The Essence (Mission/Purpose)

← Being Grounded (Objectives and action plan)

'Whoever you are, or whatever it is that you do, when you really want something, it's because that desire originated in the soul of the universe. It's your mission on earth.' (Coelho, 1993)

Creating a vision

As I mentioned before, your vision is a photograph taken in the present of what you want for yourself in the future. It identifies your values, principles and goals, providing direction to your activities and motivating you to move forward. Creating begins by stating your dreams in writing. Take your life as a whole into account, including mind, body, emotions and spirit. Consider your family, your work and social life and the world around you. Your vision should be positive and encouraging. Your natural gifts and talents are the tools that you can always rely on to make progress in life, so take into account what you most enjoy doing. Please do not allow the way you interpret your current situation to limit your ideas, because, as so many people have said "There is only one thing that makes a dream impossible and that is the fear of failure". Once you have declared your vision and outlined your mission (purpose), you can continue, working on the near future by means of short term objectives and your corresponding plan of action. Then share your personal vision with your partner because two have a greater power to make things come true than one alone. The difference between a dream and a vision is that a dream is hypothetical, remaining in thoughts and words, whereas the writing of a vision opens a pathway to follow. "The function of a vision is to inspire and provide guide lines in times of crisis".

Shared vision
When we create a vision, we have the feeling that we are co-creators of our future and not just part of something that is happening to us. If we don't know where we want to go, soon enough we can find ourselves in uncomfortable places and with people whom we didn't want to be with. Talking of people, 'There are three types of people: those who let things occur, those who make them occur and then those who ask themselves what happened'. You have to decide which group you belong to and then accept the responsibility for your decision. Being a visionary is having the inner power to change and create the world around you. When partners create a shared vision, they are linking the two individual visions. This link will strengthen what they have in common. It also helps them to be aware of their differences and, if necessary, agree to differ.

Conscious interaction
A relationship will grow in a functional way and be based on deep

foundations when the shared and chosen pathway is clear to both of the partners. Two people, each with their individual uniqueness, working side by side towards a shared vision will have access to a broader range of capabilities. Together they can build a world of creativity, productivity and fun. They will also run into areas of conflict which the shared vision will help them to resolve. The reason that we create our personal vision and then create a shared vision together with our partner is to take us to conscious interaction and this is the objective of Conscious Relationship and Intimacy.

Principles and values

The vision is grounded on principles and values. By implying them, or by making specific reference to them, they affirm the integrity of the vision. To make it possible to put our vision into practice and not just get stuck with the dream, we must clearly express in it the things that we value, what we believe in and what are the principles that we adhere to, that govern our lives.

Values are traditional, cultural and Individual. For example: cleanliness, orderliness, punctuality, dependability, achievement, discipline, obedience, sincerity, politeness, faithfulness, thrift, entertainment, recreation, independency, knowledge, etc.

Principles are universal. For example: love, justice, freedom, contact, trust, touch/sex, respect and meaning.

Conduct and behaviour

In a couple's relationship, people will always be facing trans-cultural issues, even when both are from the same country or same city. Both partners will have had different life experiences and different ways that they perceived those experiences. These differences will be manifested in the conducts and behaviours of each individual and the way in which they attribute different levels of importance to the same value. This is why it is necessary to communicate and share the content of your personal vision with your partner. By openly comparing the two personal visions, the partners will see which attitudes they share and where they differ. This important knowledge about each other will bring them closer together and enable a deeper understanding of where possible friction is likely to come from.

Completion of duties
Duties are all the things that need doing to enable us to function as a family. For the couple, there will usually be a natural distribution, some duties fit well because they are related to our personal talents and capabilities, but there are always those tasks that nobody particularly likes and their completion can easily become a source of conflict between the partners, unless there exists a clear and shared vision and we have the ability to make such an agreement and go through with it. The components of a vision are there because they are valued by the couple.

Sources of conflict
Many of the conflictual situations in a couple will stem from misunderstandings due to the different levels of importance attributed to a particular value or principle. These levels influence how we see the world around us and how we prioritise. The differences in importance levels will be behind the limiting behaviour patterns that appear in the relationship and which, in reaction, trigger defence mechanisms. By talking about the values and discussing these incidents, each member of the couple will see what they can accept and what they can't, confirm what is highly valued and what can be tolerated or ignored. There will be negotiation. Discussion will help to clarify the reasons underlying the levels of importance and whether these levels can be adjusted in the search for agreement in the process of change.

Joyful sailing

All the way along this journey toward a conscious relationship, vision, values and principles will be present, guiding the partners in their decisions as to how they intend to travel, where they want to go to and in achieving what they want. These vital elements contribute to joyful sailing, the sharing of entertainment and hobbies, the resolution of conflicts and the deepening of intimacy.

Towards Goal Accomplishment

With the perspective of your vision and the passion of your purpose or mission, we focus on the intensity and precision of your objectives.

Many leaders have shown humanity the way out of times of trouble. You are the leader of your own life and there is no mystery to it. Effective leaders have goals and result-oriented programmes.

You have something inside that motivates you to make your dreams come true. Remember that motivation is the inner drive that compels you to accomplish something and this drive never dies, it is constantly being reborn. According to David McClelland, people are motivated either to achievement, to belong / affiliation or to gain power, either personally or socially speaking.

The inner drive or balanced motivation to achieve something is what leads the individual to set challenging and demanding goals and objectives that will lead him/her step by step through the achievement of these goals and the search for excellence, with the awareness of where he/she is and where he/she is going.

From Worrying to Effective Resolution

The fact that you work with well-planned goals should in no way limit you to working just with matters that you are concerned about. To visually understand this in a simple way, I recommend you do the following exercise that is based on the teachings of Stephen Covey:

Make a list of all of the things that you are worried or concerned about and number them. For example:

1. My health
2. My financial situation
3. My future with the company
4. My brother's inconsistency
5. My mother's health
6. The polluted beaches
7. My children's education
8. My brother caring for parents
9. My cousin being out of work
10. Finishing my career
11. Hunger in Africa
12. Insecurity
13. Having a new boss
14. Not enough time for myself
15. My investments
16. etc

Draw two circles, one inside of the other. In the zone between the inner and the outer circles (called the ZONE OF CONCERN), write the number of each of the things in your list that you are concerned about but about which there is nothing that you can do (the more you worry, the less you act). It's not a question of being selfish but simply because there are matters that you cannot or should not dedicate your time or energy to (because they don't directly concern you).

CONCERN

INFLUENCE

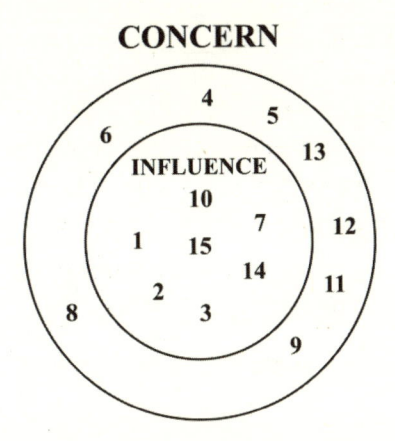

Now in the area inside the innermost circle (called the ZONE OF INFLUENCE) you jot down the numbers of the things in your list over which you feel you have influence and, moreover, that it is up to you to solve. As you set about resolving the things that can be done in the short and medium term, you will find yourself connecting little by little with other long-term matters that have appeared to be beyond your reach. In other words, it will be a lot more complicated to work for a cause like hunger in Africa when you have other more immediate unresolved matters to deal with (health, career, relationship, etc.) than when these circles are moving or closed.

Consider the following

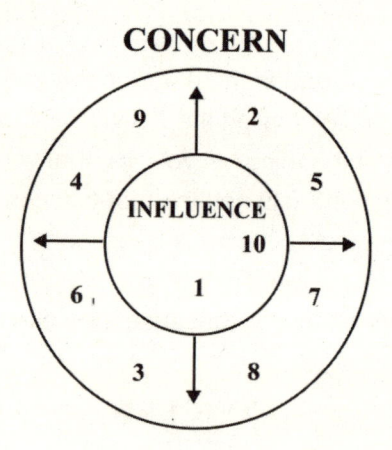

CONCERN

(Diagram: two concentric circles. Outer ring labeled CONCERN contains numbers 9, 2, 4, 5, 6, 7, 3, 8. Inner circle labeled INFLUENCE contains numbers 10 and 1. Arrows point outward in four directions.)

The more you focus your efforts on things over which you have no control, (someone else's concern for the time being), the more your energy gets dispersed and wasted and you achieve very little or no effective result at all. Actions without approach or direction give very little reward and can be highly frustrating.

The Healing Process of Shared Vision

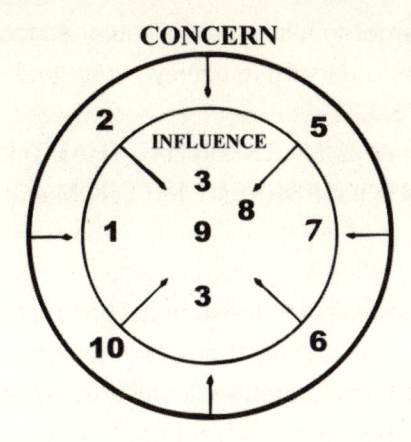

```
        CONCERN
      ┌────────┐
   2  │INFLUENCE│  5
      │   3    │
      │      8 │
   1  │ 9      │  7
      │   3    │
  10  │        │  6
      └────────┘
```

The more you focus on things you can do something about here and now, the more appropriately you use your energy. This in turn gets recycled and reinforced because effective achievement is a stimulus and it nourishes the mind and soul. Success attracts more success. By complying with your areas of influence and having your needs met, you acquire more energy and can access creativity more easily to take care of other matters in your circle of concern in an orderly and appropriate way.

Goal-Setting

One sets a goal in order to fulfil a need. You need to ask yourself two key questions before trying to achieve your goal:
1. WHY DO I NEED...?
2. WHAT TASKS ARE SO ESSENTIAL THAT THEIR NON-COMPLETION WILL PREVENT ME FROM ACHIEVING MY GOAL?

When you have the answers to these questions and you are satisfied with them, you can then state your goal.

A goal must be clear and precise, it must represent an attainable challenge and it must be measurable, both in terms of scale and the time it will take for the goal to be attained, which serves as an indicator of how the process is being handled. It is better to state your goals in writing that having them wander around loosely in your mind. Use active and appropriate words when stating your goal. The more aligned your goal is with your Purpose in Life, the easier and more enjoyable it will be to put into action and achieve.

As I mentioned before, one sets a goal in order to fulfil a need but it is not enough to merely state your goal. You need to plan in order to achieve it, for otherwise you may fall into the vicious circle of wasting energy in vain and of never doing anything to make your wish come true. The way to turn a vicious circle into a virtuous circle is by using your talents and attributes to make strategic plans of action.

The essential thing about a virtuous circle is that the goal resolves the need that you state in the CIRCLE OF ACHIEVEMENT, as follows.

It is essential to begin by making an objective DIAGNOSIS of the situation you find yourself in. Firstly, recognise that your situation is made up of **'wanting to be, having to be and what there is'**. (Adapted from Neida J. Guasamucare).

Omit any of these elements and you will become unaware of the holistic nature of reality and act merely on the basis of a subjective reality, which will give rise to ineffective results.

OBJECTIVE REALITY

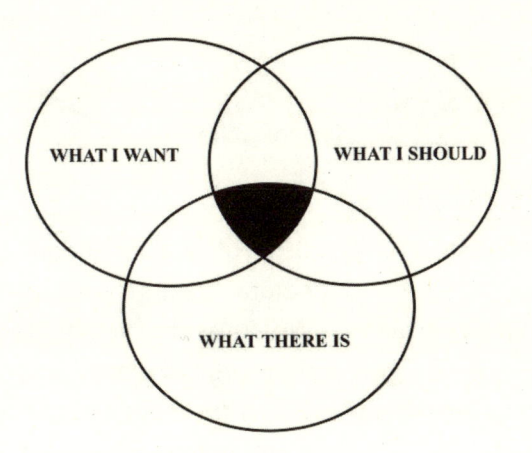

Venn diagram with three overlapping circles labelled WHAT I WANT, WHAT I SHOULD, and WHAT THERE IS.

The second thing is to make a diagnosis of what resources are available to you or not and what the obstacles are that may prevent you from achieving your goals.

CIRCLE OF ACHIEVEMENT

Assessment

Strengths
Weaknesses

Opportunities
Threats

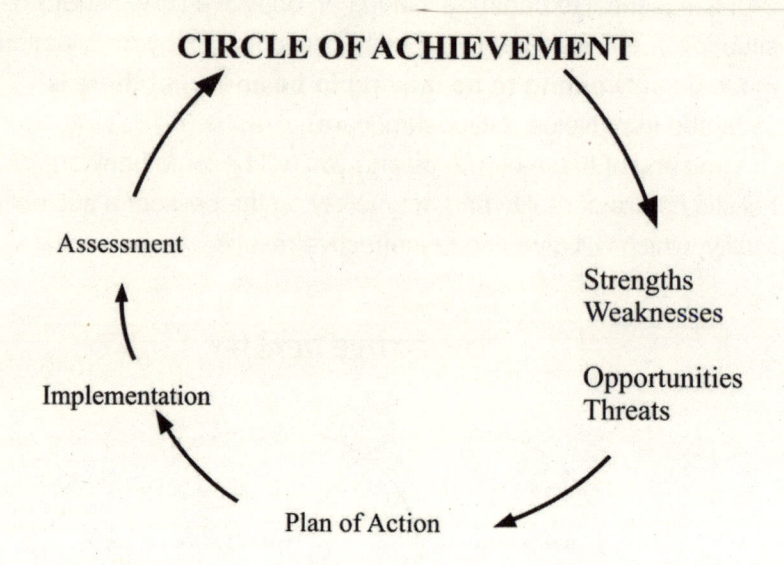

Implementation

Plan of Action

Your interior resources	**Strengths**: your attributes and natural talents
The internal obstacles	**Weaknesses**: your fears and limiting negative thoughts
Your external resources	**Opportunities:** everything that your surroundings provide you with and that stimulate you to do something
The external obstacles	**Threats:** things outside of yourself that can restrain or prevent you from achieving something

Evaluating which resources, you have and the obstacles that may be in the way renders the process of achievement more real and easier to complete. In the same way that you can enhance your strengths to increase your self-esteem and take advantage of opportunities to make the best use of particular moments in time, you also need to know what your weaknesses are and if possible, what hazards you may have to face. You can't pretend to hide from these or to ignore them because by working on your strengths, you invariably touch on your weaknesses as well in the end. If you don't state them clearly, however, they can rear their head unexpectedly and sabotage your goals. You will also lose an important opportunity to work on them. In other words, you can use your strengths to reduce any threats that may appear. If you aren't aware of them, they can hold you back or even prevent your goal from being achieved. By acknowledging your strengths and weaknesses, opportunities and threats, you will become more mature and able to recognise how you are doing, where you are and where you are headed.

If you don't know where you're going, you may end up somewhere you don't want to be.

The next thing to do is to make a PLAN OF ACTION. Planning means; **what you are going to do, how, where, when, with whom, how often, etc**. It is essential that your plan of action has more than five stages (if a difficulty arises with one, you'll have another to carry out). Also, set a date for finishing each stage. Once you have designed the plan of action, it is important to check whether all of the internal and external obstacles are in the corresponding stage so you can transform or at least minimise their effect. It is likewise essential to assess which stage will be the most difficult or the one that you least like the idea of having to do. This can be the one that you carry out first to strengthen your willpower and to avoid falling into the trap of leaving it until the end or of not doing it at all.

Implementing the Plan is the action in itself. The evaluation and the plan of action (parts one and two of the achievement cycle) refer to the thoughtful and creative yet passive part of the planning process. Actually, carrying it out is the active part. Note that the Why? is established first, then the Goal is defined and stated, followed by the design of the Plan of Action (using your resources and internal and external obstacles) and then finally comes the Implementation. You establish the time you need to carry it out in the goal. It is crucial to keep your objective in mind whilst the plan is being implemented (first things first) and to be flexible so you can deal with the interplay among the different internal and external variables.

Whilst the plan is in the process of being carried out and when it finally comes to an end, you need to make a thoughtful ASSESSMENT of it. Assessing what you have or have not achieved helps you to stay aware of yourself and your circumstance and offers the possibility of being able to continually improve.

Each goal that is diagnosed, planned, implemented and assessed is a closed circle in your life. Psychologically speaking, a mature person is one that has the ability to understand, accept and act as a consequence of the circles that he/she is continually and consciously opening, completing and closing. Hence there are no open, unattended circles and thus no leaks of energy. More to the point, the person's energy will be focused on their virtuous circles, which is the sure way to success.

It is your intention and commitment that make the difference. Whatever you do without any intention isn't done, even though it would appear to be.

The diagram or map that our minds and hearts express and that becomes tangible through material things, people and the situations in our lives, was and is created by repeating the same lines over and over again. Thought is repetitive and its law is repetition, to such a degree in fact that to transform certain results, it is necessary to do this in both the thought and action of the Law. If you think that some things are repeated, you're right because the following five headings are meant to reinforce what has been said up until now. The intention for you to make the changes that we want to make in your life come real through repetition.

Forgiveness

As I mentioned in chapter four, forgiveness is a conscious way of purifying and changing any thought, emotion or feeling that alienates you from your divine essence.

Your power to understand things, to carry them out, to complete them and to move on is situated in your divine essence. When our energy gets channelled through fear, judgement and resentment, this power becomes impaired. Forgiveness frees us from that which has mistakenly occupied this space.

Forgiving ourselves and others is a way of loving and approving of ourselves and it is from here that compassionate love arises (compassion being a combination of Love, Understanding and Acceptance).

Forgiveness releases you, for when you forgive, you no longer need a place to hide nor a mask to hide your guilt and shame at not having achieved what was expected of you.

Include the 'forgiveness process' explained in the first chapter in your exercises if you want to achieve your goals completely.

Gratitude

In addition to everything that I mentioned in chapter of Personal Law, a way of using gratitude that will strengthen your willpower and confidence in harmoniously achieving your goals is as follows:

Write down 21 things that you yourself have achieved:

Be:
Do:
Have:
For example:

I am now a mother (father), recognised professionally, healthy, an aware daughter, a great sister, a good friend, a visionary, more careful, an understanding partner, a businesswoman, etc.

I have a (or various) career(s), I have learned to speak two foreign languages, a mastery of 'x', written a book, abilities in (a sport), an excellent relationship with my partner (friends, brother/sister, work, etc.), I've learned to listen more attentively, meditate, art, etc.

I have my own house, a car, a home, a company, shares in a club, shares on the stock market, an object 'x', a musical instrument etc.

When you have all 21, keep adding more and you will realise all of the things that you have been able to be, do and obtain. This will clearly show you your power to achieve things.

Be grateful to both everything that you have achieved in the past and that which you will achieve in the future. Give the present moment a gift of gratitude (Give the present a present!).

Breathing

Breathing is an essential, biological act and it is synonymous with life. It is the first thing we do when we are born and the last before passing away. It is the source of all of our power in the physical world. It is something that is so automatic and instinctive that we often go about our lives without realising that it is an active function in the body and that we depend on it to live. We are usually so unconscious of our breathing, however, that we don't realise how much it is affected by our emotions. When we are happy we breathe fully, whereas a negative emotion can limit our breathing to such a degree that it causes the inhibition of many actions of holistic benefit to us. Most of the time, instead of breathing, we are merely sub-breathing or breathing just the minimum necessary to stay alive. It's like driving a powerful car in first gear all of the time. The bulk of the potential gets held back until we learn how to change gear.

'Achieving mastery over breathing and thought is to achieve mastery over human consciousness.' (Orr et al, 1998)

This knowledge is as old as the history of man. The first breathing techniques were developed thousands of years ago and many cultures around the world are familiar with the use of breathing as a means of transformation. The start of a new holistic understanding and approach to the human psyche came at the end of the nineteen sixties when medicine and transpersonal psychology began to use breathing as a methodology for healing.

The brain is fed by oxygen brought to it by the circulation of blood that has previously absorbed this supply of oxygen as it is pumped through the lungs by the beating of the heart. Breathing exercises and disciplines increase this oxygen supply. The exercises, both in their ancestral and modern forms are proven ways of accessing one's inner self for they are simple, safe and easy, and powerful at the same time.

Breathing consciously in a simple way is refreshing to the mind and body. Conscious breathing refreshes the vital energy in your body, it cleanses the nervous and circulatory systems, it nourishes your cells and internal organs of the body, and it cleanses and balances the body's aura.

Since the early seventies, Leonard Orr has taught by way of his own example and through repetition that 'Conscious Breathing is a practice and not just an awareness.'

Breathing is safe; living life to the full is safe!

Breathing in a conscious, connected way is like voyaging within the realm of being beyond words.

Visualisation

Visualisation is a powerful ally for maximising the human being's unlimited potential. The support elements are conscious breathing, key words and expressions (affirmation) and poetry, colour (including symbols and diagrams), flower essences, specific types of music and essential oils. A key word or expression is essential for activating the memory while colours, flowers and essential oils enable one to be more creative and limitless (colours can be calming to the brain just like certain types of music). These elements awaken the holistic consciousness in the brain.

Thought works through repetition and it is for this reason that it is so powerful. You convey your mind and energy to whatever it is you are focusing on, you repeat it constantly on both the conscious and unconscious levels and you manifest it. **BELIEVING IS CREATING**. By imitating this same process and combining it with the key elements (conscious breathing, words, colour, flowers, essential oils and symbols and supported at times with a certain type of music), you visualise what you want and how to get it in a clear, simple and enjoyable way. What you achieve is a meaningful image that is easy to imagine and repeat that serves as the scale model in your mind that you need and can use immediately to start manifesting it in your normal, tangible reality.

The Holistic Collage

A holistic collage is similar to a photograph of the future created in the present. To make one, take a sheet of cardboard and some paper, colours markers, crayons, paintbrushes. From a selection of magazines, cut out images that portray your vision and goals. Find photographs, poetry and any other visual element that are inspiring to you. Fix these to the collage sheet to create a visual story.

Developing the collage is just like setting goals but in this case, it is a goal that you set by using visual creativity. It should be a challenge for you and at the same time achievable and clear in its message. It should enable you to measure your progress, as every time you look at the holistic collage, it will activate your positive thinking, stimulated by the visualisation process. Every time you visualise what you want, the ideas expressed in the holistic collage develop and become closer to reality.

There are three key steps to making a successful holistic collage:

1 Give thanks instead of asking for what you desire. Write across the top of the collage: 'I (your name) am grateful for all of this'. This is a way of recognising that we are co-creators of our life.

2 After assembling your holistic collage and before signing, connect with your heart and mind and write at the bottom: 'This, or something better, manifests for me here and now, in harmony with everybody involved and the universe. Thank you' followed by your signature and date.

3 Prepare the holistic collage in a conscious and dedicated way, but be detached from your results. This way, you allow yourself the space to be able to give particular attention to the trust that you have in yourself and in the universe as a whole. You will learn about acceptance and how to handle the undertow of your longings. Imagine that you are an artist inspired with the work you have at hand. Experience and enjoy the whole process regardless of the end result, connecting the conception of the idea to its development and completion and even beyond the finishing of the piece. Once a work of art is created, it generates a force and acquires a life of its own.

Be grateful, joyful and aware when making your holistic collage. Be efficient and determined to achieve your goal and accept your results. Remember: you always get whatever you need for your higher evolution and development.

Meditation, taking care of the seed that you have planted

Once you have the image firmly in your mind (the VISUALISATION) and on paper (the HOLISTIC COLLAGE), it is also essential to 'care for the seed that you have planted so that it germinates and grows well' (affirmation or the eternal law). You need to create an appropriate space where you can learn to still the mind so that there is a pause between one thought and the next. This way, you can enhance the image of what you want (your vision).

How can you achieve this? Wearing loose, comfortable clothing, choose a quiet place where you can sit in a chair with your feet firmly on the floor. If you prefer to sit on the floor, use a cushion so that you can fold your legs in such a way that they support your body. If necessary, put cushions under your knees as well. Whether you are sitting in a chair or on the floor, keep your back as straight as possible without it getting stiff. It is important to be as comfortable as possible. Put your hands on your thighs, close your eyes and focus on your breathing. Inhale deeply and evenly and breathe out slowly with every breath. You can also listen to music that you enjoy when doing this. Don't stay with your thoughts, observe them and let them pass by. Stay focused on your breathing by using an affirmation. The length of time you spend meditating is not critical, the important is to make it a regular practice. However, you will find that it gets progressively longer until the time you spend is appropriate for you.

By repeating the meditation – visualization exercises process and everything involved with it over and over again, your achievements in life gain ground. You'll find your mind and heart lighter because you have come to live the present moment as a gift, your past limitations will become transformed and the future becomes that which you truly deserve.

The Continual Process of Making a Dream Come True:

Dream	+	Idealised Action	=	Vision
Vision	+	Directed Action	=	Mission/Purpose
Mission	+	Planned Action	=	Goal
Goal	+	Creative Action	=	Holistic Collage
Holistic Collage	+	Effective Action	=	Success

Humankind's potential is limitless. It just needs time, energy and space for it to expand.

Dreaming of your own future will enable you to create it better. Create your own future because you don't want others creating it for you.

Harvesting the fruit

Albert Einstein said that 'the important problems that we face cannot be resolved on the same level that we create them.' Self-knowledge, together with the creativity to use our special gifts and talents and a master programme that is based on joy and well-being, will lead to the resolution of critical situations in our lives. **By assuming the responsibility for our existence and actions**, we can develop potential areas for improvement.

The point of balance in the holistic development of an individual is found by focusing on the three cycles of the person's life:

DEVELOPING AND MAINTAINING AN AWARENESS OF SUCCESS MEANS:
CLEARING THE PAST AND PUTTING IT IN ORDER.
PASSIONATELY LIVING THE PRESENT,
CREATING THE FUTURE THAT ONE DESERVES.

As every circle that is connected and being developed is put in order, it leads us to the next one. If you get stuck in a particular area or patch of your life, you face the possibility of being paralysed and seeing your creativity worn down by obsession and ineffectiveness.

Having cleared your past and eliminated or minimised the trauma related with it, you will be able to integrate it into your life. As you experience the present moment and its consequences as a true gift of life, you will also find yourself pleasantly surprised and even amazed by the events in your life. Your experience of the past may serve you as a reference but will not limit you as a person moving continuously as energy because you know that the present moment is the gift of life. In this way, you will develop the skill to both prevent certain situations and to handle uncertainty with an attitude based on conscious learning and teaching. From the awareness of gratitude that comes from living one day to the next, it becomes easy and normal to do what you do with joy and love, as is your privilege and responsibility to do so, and to create a brilliant and abundant future, giving and receiving everything that you deserve.

KNOWING HOW AND WHERE YOU ARE AND WHERE YOU ARE GOING...
KNOWING WHAT TO USE TO GET WHERE YOU WANT TO GO...
WITH THIS AWARENESS, NOTHING CAN STOP YOUR SUCCESS.

BEING + DOING + ACHIEVING = SUCCESS

'When one does what one is supposed to be doing, the whole universe conspires to provide you with what you need.' (Coelho, 1993)

According to Carl G. Jung 'Consciousness is a very recent acquisition of nature and it is still in an experimental stage'. Cherish your awareness of Being and Doing as part of the infinite global consciousness.

Intuition is what most stands out as you expand your global consciousness as part of the process of holistic growth. A combination of instinct and discernment, it is the discernment or wisdom that distinguishes us from other living beings. Instinct provides you with an indication, a yearning, a group of possibilities while discernment provides you with the structure, the ability to assess, and the form and purpose. Instinct and discernment combine together and as they transform, you add a touch of imagination and then you begin to see sparks of opportunity that, when they are kindled, can lead to flourishing of the most creative types of work.

Achieving the dream
In summary, to achieve our dream relationship, we need to know ourselves well and be familiar with what is in our heart. We should develop awareness, both of our own values and the values of anyone with whom we are considering intimately sharing our life, not only listening to what we say about ourselves but also observing how we actually model those beliefs, how we act them out in our lives. It will be just as important to patiently observe how the partner acts out their values. The relationship will be stronger and healthier if these practical, day to day values are held in common with the chosen partner. The lack of balance in these values should be a subject of discussion, as you search for ways to resolve the differences and come to solid agreements. To follow this process is

just as essential to partners before commitment as it is to those who have been in a committed relationship for a long time.

Achieving a shared vision in 7 steps

1- Create your own vision
2- Your partner creates his/hers
3- Enjoy the process of finding common elements in your visions
4- Create a shared vision
5- Create action plans to achieve your shared vision
6- Keep dreaming and expanding individually and together
7- Enjoy the process based in shared core values and principles

Crossing the Ocean

On your way down the river of life
To the delta where the brown meets the blue
Be as vast, unlimited and bountiful as the ocean.
As you lap at the shore gently rocking with the breeze

Remember your power to rage
Be a whirlwind with your tempest.
You can be deep and calm,
Swelling and rolling with majestic wave
Or shallow and treacherous,
Ripping and foaming with tide
Recall your power of choice.
You can stretch forever,
Meet the sky at the horizon
And become the white clouds.

You can go to extremes,
Float around the planet
Frozen like a 'berg
But do not forget what joy
To melt and dissolve in the heat.

All these transformations are within your power.
Let go, trust in the one.
Be open to your destiny,
For an ocean refuses no river,
We are but sand tumbled on the beach.

Who Makes the Bed?

Chapter Eight
The Couple as Successful Business Partners

This subject has formed part of my theoretical and practical experience in the field of Holistic Organizational Consultancy since 1993. I write about this in different media and give lectures and lead academic trainings. The results of this very active work in both Venezuela and Cyprus, countries where I have lived for many years, and other international work are to be published in a new book.

The loving partners in business
One of the major problems in family businesses is that the couple starts up the business themselves. They will use their own knowledge, experience, love, will, motivation, drive and financial resources. This is all wonderful and all those elements set in motion the vision. However, there is a huge drain of material and human resources in the first years because many family businesses lose sight of the fact that they need more than the basic administrative and managerial qualities to run the business. In many examples, the couple, with all their love and motivation don't have those qualities, so they have to outsource them. To obtain the help they need they must be aware of their strengths and weaknesses and which are the skills that are lacking.

Having the guidance of a holistic business coach-consultant is always an essential support. Never more so than during the Start-Up phase. The resources invested in consultancy at the beginning of a business are as important as securing the right premises and the material resources. Every hour spent in holistic coaching at the beginning will save you days and weeks of problems in the future. The business consultant is the one that will see the whole picture and measure what the couple can count on as emotional, material and experiential resources according to the roles and tasks that the business needs in its first years of growth.

It is also fundamental that the consultant has a holistic formation, as emotional considerations are always important and especially so in a family business.

Creating business while you still work for others

My wish for you by way of this description is to recognize and accept the leader in you regardless of whether you are an employer or employee, or maybe both. A leader knows how to build a company from his/her role; all it needs is time, energy and room to achieve it, and this means purpose, attention, passion and direction.

Just like with individuals, organisations are a context where there is an ideal, a wish or a dream that a group of people strive to achieve. This ideal is described in a concept known as VISION which is nothing more than what we want to be in the future. The vision of a holistic organisation covers the whole company and the people who are connected with it. It suggests a direction for the future, a dream or a challenge that people share in common.

Having a vision of the future is fundamental for the strategic planning of an organisation.

We all form part of some kind of organisation with a vision, whether this has been stated or not. If you don't have your own personal vision of the future, it is going to be difficult to accompany a group, an organisation or a company that is progressing towards its vision of the future. If your dream is to get away from the city in seven or eight years' time, to buy a farm and to live in nature, that's fine because while you have your vision of the future in mind and in your heart in the here and now, you will be aligned with your vision and giving the very best of yourself in your job so that your dream comes true. The point is that in having your own vision, the more you strive for it the more you support the company in its vision and the faster and more dynamically and harmoniously the company reaches its vision, the better it will be for you, too. The organization where you are now, wants you to give the best of yourself here and now so that you can get to where you want to be. If that means with the same organization, that's fine and if not, that's also fine.

Business vision
A vision of the future of an enterprise has basically the same features as individual personal vision. It needs to be formulated by the leaders and shared with its members, and it should be comprehensive and detailed, based on values and principles, and be impressive and encouraging. Maintaining a positive attitude in terms of the future is essential. According to the expert on the subject Joe Barker, 'it is the nations with a vision of the future that get the best results.' His experience as a teacher has shown him that the best students are the ones that have clear goals. The fact that this is more important than both social standing and IQ for a child to get good results is very revealing.

The approach for creating a vision of the future within the strategic business plan is similar to that for personal vision. A vision or mission is established, a diagnosis is made, the goals and the corresponding plans of action are defined, and the process is carried out and assessed, i.e. the results and their cost are evaluated.

The gift of a clear vision
A vision of the future is an essential aspect of the individual and of an organisation. In the individual, it is represented by the spiritual dimension or sense of meaning, whereas in an organisation it is represented by the strategy and function of the enterprise.

A vision of the future should thus point to your destiny or that of the organisation. It is not so much a question of figures but more of the consequences of having achieved your goals. By focusing on figures, all you achieve is a very narrow-minded approach. The important thing is to see things in their broadest sense because this way, the figures will multiply in the end. With a vision of the future, the power is in your hands. Do you want to be a mere observer or an active part of your life and the world? No one can condemn you if you want to be an observer although this will have its consequences and you will have to accept them. The choice is yours whether to just float or to swim in the ocean of life. 'Each one of us needs to find his/her own starfish, and if we all put them back wisely and carefully, the 21st century will be a better place and time to live. (Adapted from The Star Thrower Story by Joel Barker)

Dreaming of your own future will enable you to create it better. Create your own future because you don't want others creating it for you.

Precious tools to evaluate you and your business
According to Ichak Adizes, each of the points mentioned below corresponds to a function that makes an organisation effective.

A holistic organisation is a group of people, whether it be a business or not, that achieves balanced effectiveness by consciously taking care of all of the different elements involved, including the people, processes, structure, strategies and rewards, all within the context of a permanent interaction where whatever happens to one affects the other, either supporting or restraining it.

A vision of the future is sustained by values that are the heart of the energy flow in an organisation for they establish the correctness of the path that is chosen.

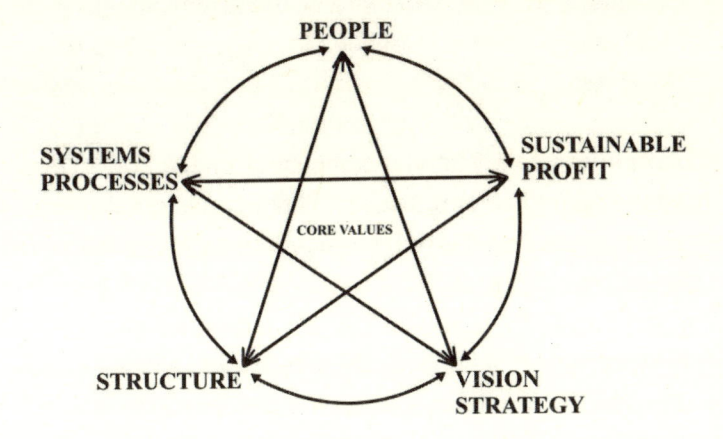

```
              PEOPLE
               ↑↑
SYSTEMS       / \       SUSTAINABLE
PROCESSES ←──────→      PROFIT
         \ CORE VALUES /
          \           /
   STRUCTURE        VISION
                    STRATEGY
```

From the transpersonal point of view, a holistic team, family, organization even a country fits Dr. Ichak Adizes' **PAEI** model of Management styles. It is very appropriate for it complies with the four dimensions of effectiveness or the basic functions that generate indispensable results in the short and the long term:

Produce effective results: producers **(P)** What to do. The basic reason of the existence of the organization. Produce Products or Services to satisfy the need of the customer.

Administrate efficiently: administrators **(A)** how to do. How to get things organised, planned, systematized and under control by the rights procedures, processes and systems.

Entrepreneur Be constantly enterprising and adaptable to changes: Entrepreneurial people **(E)** How to innovate in ways that are in tune with their vision of the future. It requires having 'sight' and the ability to see things plus the willingness to believe in those visions and undertake significant risks.

Integrator An organisation is the result of integrating and developing people at both the personal and professional levels. Integrators **(I)** know how to create team work through people's commitment over the short, medium and long terms. Well integrated organizations have persistent culture of mutual respect and trust.

The four **PAEI** functions permanently interact. For this reason, an organisation is holistic when there are holistic leaders who understand that human effectiveness is possible when the individual is conceived as a whole which is made up of the physical, mental, emotional and spiritual bodies that are always interacting with each other

BODY | MIND
EMOTION | SPIRIT

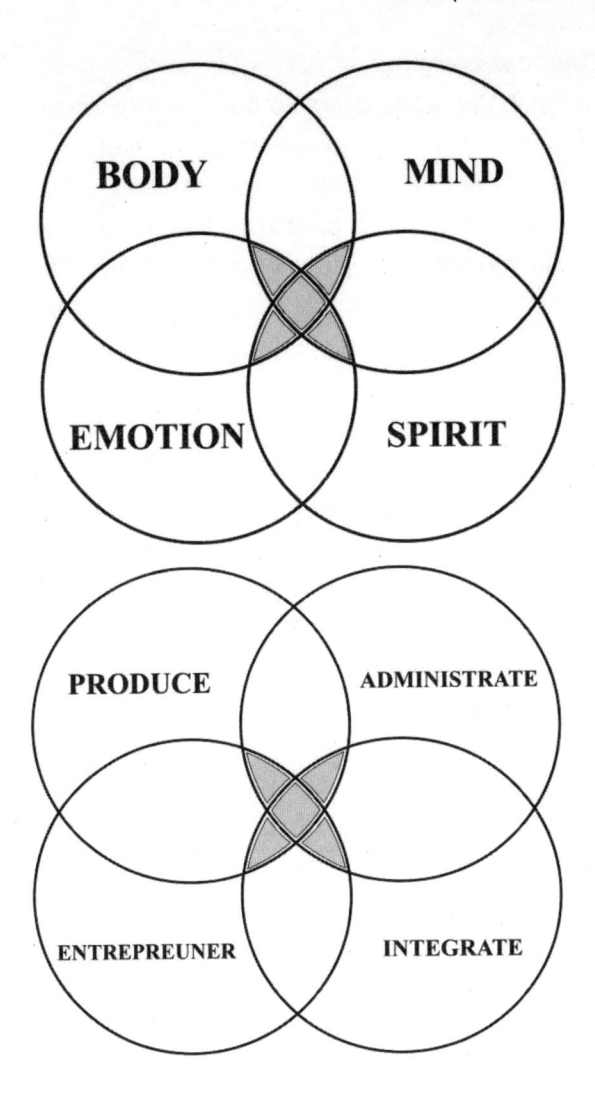

PRODUCE | ADMINISTRATE
ENTREPREUNER | INTEGRATE

Processes that are successful in strengthening and ensuring the balanced, harmonious growth of an organisation, whether it is small, medium or large-sized, public, private or involved in manufacturing or providing services, must satisfy the individual's four levels, the five dimensions of organisation and the four dimensions of effectiveness.

Humankind's Deepest Longing

'I find the great thing in this world is not so much where we stand, as in what direction we are moving: to reach the port of heaven, we must sail sometimes with the wind and sometimes against it - but we must sail, and not drift, nor lie at anchor'. (Quoted from The Autocrat of the Breakfast Table by Oliver Wendell Holmes 1858).

To sum up, we all have natural gifts and virtues. Imagination, a faculty of the mind and spirit, is one of our natural gifts and we can use it as we like. You can create a dream based on something real, like the things you have and what you like doing. It is very exciting to know that you can make a living from something that you like doing, as well as making a contribution, whether it is small or large, to the world. Business is about offering a service, a product or an idea to others who need it, and the more these services, products and ideas are connected with your natural gifts and the things you naturally like doing, the easier it will be for you to do them, the better will be your contribution and the greater will be your reward. Moreover, **humankind's deepest longing is to be useful and to be rewarded.** Everybody has this longing, whether you are an employee or employer. We all want to be useful and to be rewarded. When somebody makes the decision to start to run a business, he or she not only wants to multiply their capital, i.e. to be rewarded; they also want to be useful to others. This is why they get involved in the (not so easy) process of turning an idea into reality by creating lots of tasks and jobs and dealing with the implications of management dynamics. Company life, like life itself, is an on-going process of teaching and learning where all of us are involved, both employers and employees. By being clear on where we are and where we are going, we can definitely take best advantage of the process by acknowledging everybody's true worth. *Through the fulfilment of what each one wants individually, we all make it possible for the vision and mission of others to also be fulfilled.*

Working is not the same as honouring the work that you do. By dignifying your work with joy, acceptance and pleasure, you come to live your work as love and to love your work as life. 'Solidarity and happiness aren't always about doing what you want; they're more a matter of loving what you do'. 'Someone who doesn't know how to enjoy himself doesn't know what work is and someone who doesn't know what work is doesn't know how to enjoy himself.' (Adapted from the teaching of Dr. Juan Jose Sanchez, Traditional Chinese Medicine).

When Loving Partners cannot be business partner
In my 24 years of experience in relationship counselling and coaching including my own, it has become very evident to me that some couples even though they have a successful intimate relationship are not suited to work together at all. As it is much easier to find a business partner than an intimate loving one, it is not worth damaging the beauty of a good relationship for insisting in business join venture. Even better, if you can, let go and try again some years later. A good solid loving relationship will have a space to explore and try again and let go, all are steps into nurturing intimacy beyond the myth of "couples cannot or should not work together".

Wind kissed waves

A colonnaded basilica, spiral mosaics, a busy harbour,
Now just a confusion of wind weathered stones,
the storm scattered debris of protective walls.
Visualise the frailty of civilisation's power,
Wander the white sand dunes, littered with terra cotta.
Laze in the turquoise shallows like a turtle.

As the sulky sun spins slowly down now,
Quenched by silken seas beyond our horizons,
A festival of light and colours is thrown into the heavens.
As we swirl on past the twilight into darkness,
A serenade of wind kissed waves, tumbling onto starlit sand,
Drifts enticingly through the night.

Chapter Nine
Healing Addiction Revives Intimacy

Addiction is a persistent and irresistible desire for a particular and familiar feeling or experience. Addiction is a brain disease and it is not just a "moral insufficiency". It starts with feeling of ecstasy and untreated frequently ends with death. The afflicted person seeks to replace unbearable dullness in their life with exhilaration and they are possessed by the objective of attaining that pleasurable state of mind which enables temporary (but repeatable) escape from a physical or psychological pain they are carrying. This addictive state develops progressively through a number of levels from simple consumption, to substance abuse or obsessive habits, ending with total dependence. Addiction is one of the biggest killers of intimacy.

Dependencies
Humans are creative and over the centuries have discovered and developed many new addictive substances and processes. In spite of legislation aimed at limiting their consumption, the highly profitable return from the commercialisation of these addictive substances and activities is usually what funds and accelerates their widespread proliferation. There is a new language describing the disease of addiction, like Stance use disorder, process addiction for gambling, primary addiction, etc... The most common addictions that people suffer from are drugs, alcohol, tobacco and gambling (the idea of easy money). Then we have computer and internet addiction, sexual addictions, workaholism, shopping and eating disorders. Worldwide, alcoholism is the most common addiction, but

because those affected usually do not consider themselves 'alcoholic', they do not consider taking treatment and we do not have the real statistics. But as most hard drugs are illegal, we have much more statistical information about it and maybe, for this reason, it is considered that there are more drugs addicts than alcoholics. Even though these two addictions are typically the most common ones, nowadays, the number of the non-chemical addictions such as eating disorders (bulimia, anorexia, binge eating), gambling and new technology addictions have increased greatly. Emerging ones are the addiction to plastic surgery, internet pornography and the usually unnoticed but harmful addiction to prescription medications such as benzodiazepines and barbiturates. Every day it is more and more common to encounter people who abuse this kind of medication in order to 'get high' or to avoid pain.

The final state of failure
Those first feelings that the sufferer gets from an addiction, whether from drugs, alcohol or from some other source are flush/rapture/ecstasy. This can be described as a temporary state of consciousness where the body and mind are extremely over stimulated or under stimulated. It is often described as 'an experience of ecstasy and feelings of symbiosis with the cosmos'. As the addiction develops, the feeling is achieved more often and more easily by taking more doses or having more than one addiction. Addiction is the final state of failure in the search for the flush/rapture/ecstasy which was felt when that substance or behaviour was first experienced.

The drug of choice
Most addicts have more than one addiction; this is the way it develops and for this, therapists employ the term 'drug of choice'. Among the several addictions, this is the one that brings the patient to therapy. For example, the person that consumes heroin may

already have had a drinking habit for several years and then after they began using heroin may have reduced drinking because of the heroin consumption, though it was their drinking habit which created the need for another addiction. Another example is cocaine addiction, which almost always goes hand in hand with alcohol consumption. It is for this reason that abstinence from all addictive substances is so important for the healing process. As an addictive personality myself, and a psychotherapist, I know how difficult it can be, but it is something worth fighting for.

Different types of addiction
The treatments for different types of addictions can be divided into two major categories; the chemical addictions and the non-chemical ones. For the latter group, such as: gambling, Internet games, online chat, sex sites, Internet pornography, online shopping, TV., workaholism, eating disorders, shopping, sexaholism, kleptomania, co-dependency/love addiction and so on, our treatment will be based on coaching based and beyond 12 steps, Breathwork and psychotherapy individual and group, bodywork such as massage and Watsu and creative development such as colour and image consultancy. In some cases, we would also need medication in the early stages of treatment. For the chemical addictions, such as: alcohol, marijuana (cannabis), amphetamines, stupefients, anxiolitics, sleeping pills, the acid drugs such as cocaine, heroin, LSD, Ecstasy, opiate used in epidemic proportions, particularly in North America, etc. we need a process of the above-mentioned therapies and in addition, detoxification, vitamins, minerals and medication. In some cases, hospitalization maybe required. Cigarettes are also chemical, but they don't generate the entire abstinence syndrome like nausea, shaking, fever, extreme anxiety, sickness, sweating, etc. A high percentage of the therapeutical approaches that deal with addiction are based on the "12 step programs". Even though some drugs or behaviours (food disorders,

sex, gambling, ecstasy, etc.) by themselves don't produce the addiction, it is the effect of sensations and feelings which they provoke in some people which leads to the addiction. There are others like heroin, cocaine and LSD amongst others that will damage the reward system of the brain and this damaged area will stop producing dopamine, the lack of which will produce the chemical addiction to substitute what is missing.

Beginning the healing
The first three months of a treatment are focused on coaching the client/patient to reconnect with their resources, their capabilities and talents, as they will be quite damaged by the dependency. This would include family therapy, if possible, and transpersonal psychotherapy once a week or more if required. Group therapy is also most recommended (in the rehabilitation centres, it is a must) and then Follow up after recovery. The coaching techniques I use, employ Breathwork in order to reconnect with the force of life and willpower, Hypnosis, if required and psychotherapy. We accompany our clients on a journey with a team of complementary doctors, body workers and beauty experts. For a successful treatment, the following recommendations would be followed: Abstinence from all chemical addictions forever (for at least 18 months), The Removal of all addictive substances from the house, The Avoidance of persons who were involved in the addiction and the Rituals of the addictions.

Family support
It is important that family members should be co-opted into the healing process, there are diverse options to follow. Also, family members should be co-opted into the healing process and should take care not to consume (e.g. alcohol) in the presence of the addict. The availability of support from family and friends as well as professional support is crucial to success as during the healing

process while the addict begins to feel more secure, they will risk trying to show their power over the addiction (e.g. an alcoholic will make an appointment in a bar or will cook with brandy). One of the most important and valuable factors in the rehabilitation of the addict is the participation of the family group. Family can continue to do their progressive work even if the client opts not to engage or cease their treatment.

Identifying the severity
The first step is the recognition of the problem. This realisation can come from within or from a loved one who is prepared to spell out the truth. Once the usual period of denial has been overcome, a specialist can be consulted to evaluate and decide if the situation is one of addicted-dependent, abuser or consumer.

The consumers are just one step from becoming addicted. The difference between a consumer and an addict is that the consumer can pass some time without consuming and this situation will not alter their life. For example, if a person consumes alcohol only if they are dinning out, then they will try to dine out frequently, every weekend and maybe a night in middle of the week and they would spend energy creating the situations to do so. BUT, if for any reason, they couldn't dine out, then they will not consume alcohol and that will not affect their behaviour or their sleep or resting time. However, they will be looking forward to consuming again as they have already established a ritual.

The highly consumer is simply in a prior stage to becoming an addict. They have already created the tendency and when they are faced with more difficult or challenging situations they can easily jump to the addiction level. The abuser is the type of consumer who, every time they consume, does it in high doses or frequently. They are unable to regulate the quantity or time. The addicted or dependant person, in the same example of drinking alcohol, drinks a high quantity every day and feels that they cannot function without it. They depend on the alcohol to be able to function. They develop: loss of control, withdrawal symptoms, inability to abstain, compulsion of repeating, increasing the dose for more effect, dispersion of interests, social descent, psychological and physical ruin.

Take the example of addiction to smoking. If cigarettes don't cause the cancer of: trachea, oesophagus, larynges, throat, tongue, palate, lungs, certainly it is a huge aggravation and yet some people in treatment for those conditions still continue to smoke. The sane person is the one that doesn't consume on a regular basis, or doesn't do it at all.

Causes of addiction

The exact reason why people go to addiction is still a mystery. What we do know however, is that it is inherited but it is not clear if it is genetic or if it is a learnt behaviour. Statistics show that almost all addicts have a family member who is addicted.

Maybe not all of them have the same addiction but the weakness to addiction exists, even if the addict didn't personally meet that member of the family. There is usually a certain secrecy about addicted people that has been perceived by the newly addicted. Even when we cannot assure that there is a genetic bond between an addicted parent and an addicted child, we can be assured that it is a frequent occurrence.

A way of preventing addiction

According to David Lamus, expert in the subject of addiction; "There has been much money, time and energy invested in educating and informing communities about the risks of consuming addictive substances without significantly favourable results. A better result can be created by assertive communication involving a proportional amount of information together with personal and emotional experience. This recipe produces better results in creating a consciousness in the community. Nowadays the method with the best results is the one developed by William R Miller and Stephen Rollnick, which combines a mix of cognitive-behavioural therapy (directive) with client-based therapies (evocative) in which the client is shown the possible risks and contradictions of his or her behaviour but he or she is allowed to develop their own conclusions and configure the options of their treatment". I will add Breathwork to this formula and it will increase enormously the power of the method.

In conclusion
A recovery person can have a happy, joyous, productive and meaningful life. I am one of them and I have seen and worked with many clients that have achieved such positive outcomes.
I also believe that someone who is involved in developing an awareness of their own values and is content with the current situations in their lives will have a much greater resistance to the lure of addictions and will have the wisdom and the courage when necessary to leave a relationship with an addict. Therapy, coaching and bodywork will build up self-esteem, provide helpful guidance and facilitate the resolution of stressful personal situations. This is the creation of a resilient 'immune system' capable of preventing and healing addiction.

7 Steps for awareness and action

1. Evaluate and share what you think about your addiction or your partner's as soon as possible. Remember that addicts lie and deny and spend a lot of energy trying to convince you that 'the other guy' is the one responsible and guilty of their behaviour
2. Communicate your feelings and findings. Remember that addicts are the ones who lose their inner freedom, willpower and motivation to change.
3. Ask for professional help for both - the addict and their partner/family member (co-addicted). Addicts cannot manage even a small level of anxiety, they go to addiction to compensate.
4. May love be present in the whole process. Caring for oneself and the one who needs to heal the addiction is a challenging task. Remember that you may love the person and hate their addictive behaviour.
5. Love and forgiveness doesn't necessarily mean staying in a damaging relationship. Make the decisions adequately and on time. Addiction is a physical, moral and spiritual illness.
6. Ask friends and family for support. Addicts are ego driven, they lack self-confidence and self-worth, they suffer from mood swings and depression.
7. Remember that a process of change and rehabilitation is long and hard, it takes time, energy and space.

Desolation

Slouched on a snow-covered bench,
Buttocks melting and wet,
The empty park encircled by black railings.
Eyes buried deep within dark rings of tiredness,
Her hair a sorry mess, the winter ruthlessly cruel,
Her meagre clothing too thin for comfort.

Loneliness lines the beaten withered face.
Yearning to share her joy at news of a distant birth.
She will send the desolate selfie image to a virtual face,
Along with her crumpled dreams.
A mother's relationship that never matured,
Failed to hold them together.
The wasted toil crying out of an empty life.

Who Makes the Bed?

Chapter Ten
The Rhythm of the Breath

Stress is a state of inner personal anxiety and can occur in all aspects of our lives. It triggers processes of non-communication that hinder productivity, creativity and intimacy. All of us, in some way or another, can be affected by this 'condition'. Symptoms like bad moods, prolonged tiredness, anxiety, lack of motivation and negative vision are almost normal in today's world, yet prolonged exposure to them will create serious unbalance in our systems. A major difficulty of healing this 'illness' lies in the fact that stress continuously feeds back on itself. Once it is present in the organism, its effect becomes a cause. It is important to differentiate between what I call "Creative Tension" and "Real Stress". Creative Tension is a stressful situation where we retain a certain control, such as in sport or the organisation of a wedding. Real Stress appears in a situation where we have no control over the event, such as an accident, natural disaster, economic crisis, etc.

Stress inhibits breathing
One of the most devastating effects of stress is the inhibition of breathing. With the repetition of stressful situations, the result becomes chronic and generates serious hang-ups such as lack of creativity, low productivity, chronic fatigue and mood swings amongst others. The symptoms experienced can be repressed emotions, frustration, lack of purpose, difficulty in expressing love and gratitude, all of which will affect our access to intimacy.

In order to fully liberate ourselves from the effects of stress, the study and practice of breathing techniques is an excellent place to begin.

Breathing

Breathing is a life-sustaining activity that we begin to practice instinctively from the moment we are born and continues uninterrupted until the moment we die. The rhythm of our respiration is such a familiar practice to us that most of our lives we are even unaware of our participation in this vital action. Remember, however, that though we are able to survive for many days without food and not quite so long without water, if we are prevented from breathing, most humans will be dead within three or four minutes. This is how fundamental the breathing process is to our well-being.

Breathing dynamics

Let us take a closer look at the dynamics of the breathing process. Singers and wind instrument players, amongst others, are always conscious of breathing as their music depends on being able to deliver a continuous flow of breath across the vocal chords or through their musical instruments. Athletes depend on powerful breathing rhythms to be able to deliver high levels of oxygen to their performing muscles. The air that we inhale into our lungs contains a percentage of oxygen and when this oxygen content comes into contact with the blood circulating in the spongy tissues of our lungs, it is absorbed into the blood stream. The steady pumping of our heart supplies oxygen rich blood to our brain and to the muscles and organs of our bodies where the oxygen is consumed in an energy-supplying mission. When we are working hard our hearts beat faster and we breathe more strongly to supply the increase in energy required by our bodies. In a healthy body, this biological breathing dynamic manages itself naturally and instinctively without the requirement of any conscious intervention.

Energy levels

We are however, capable of intervening in this natural sequence by intentionally modifying the character of our breathing rhythms. For example, if we choose to breathe more strongly than usual whilst remaining physically inactive, we alter the natural supply and demand equilibrium, creating a higher than usual level of energy throughout our bodies. Research and practical experimentation with the effects of unusual body energy levels has led to the development of many physical and spiritual practices that we find in disciplines such as martial arts, tai-chi, chi-kong and yoga and meditation to name just a few, and therapeutical disciplines such as rebirthing breathwork, holotropic breathwork, integrative breathing, transformational breathwork amongst others.

Processes of transformation

The breathwork techniques in the practices of martial arts are concerned with the development of the chi so vital to success in combat. Breathing is also used in massage techniques such as shiatsu and touching hearts massage. In meditation, yoga, tai-chi and chi-kong, practices have focused more on using the inner calm created by the breathing to develop chi, awareness, presence and mindfulness. Rebirthing breathwork, also known as conscious connected breathing, adds to all the above a greater sense of self-awareness and, above all, the improvement of mental, physical and spiritual well-being, achieving a consciousness of wholeness. Both ancestral and modern practices acknowledge the importance of breathing in processes of transformation.

Rebirthing breathwork

This methodology (which is also known as Conscious Connected Breathing) is a powerful therapeutical process because of its depth, simplicity and efficiency. Rebirthing Breathwork teaches how to breathe fully, releasing emotional energy stuck in the system and clearing the pathway to holistic well-being. It was developed in the early seventies by Leonard Orr. Its major goal is to help release energy blockages caused by suppressed experiences and traumas that have been stored in the body and mind, hindering the healthy flow of breath and energy and preventing many people from breathing to their full capacity.

Rebirthing Breathwork works deeply with two very human activities, breathing and thinking. These fundamental elements help each individual to understand and accept that all the resources needed to develop their creativity and holistic potential are already within themselves. This enables the possibility of coherent actions. All we need is time, energy and space.

When working with clients, the process of Rebirthing Breathwork begins with an in-depth interview about present concerns and questioning about events of life history, somatic exploration, counselling, then 40 to 60 minutes of conscious connected breathing concluded by the sharing of feedback.

A complete initiation cycle will include 10 to 12 sessions with a professional Breathworker, enabling the client to integrate the process and be able to practice breathing sessions by themselves, even though their therapeutical process may continue.

A rebirthing breathwork session.
Through practical experience, the client learns to breathe, relax and remain aware with an attitude of acceptance. A personal inner atmosphere is created that allows repressed 'material' to come to the surface of the consciousness. Such thoughts and memories also have their emotional counterpart and a physical reference point in the body. As the associated energy is released and begins to circulate throughout the body and the mind, physical tensions are softened and eventually dissolved. Emotions are expressed and conscious decisions are made. As this physical and emotional relief is expressed, breathing becomes deeper and flows fully and

spontaneously. The client is assisted to resolve and integrate past experiences and to progressively release the old traumas and develop a breath that circulates easily and freely.

The rhythm of the breath

We find that it takes considerable motivation and willpower to breathe steadily and rhythmically for extended periods whilst remaining physically inactive. The mental effort of full lung inflation, along with balanced flows of inhale and exhale, leaves little room in the thought process of the mind for any of our habitual chit-chat brain activity. This situation of focus can create emptiness in the mind similar to the void experienced with the lengthier breathing rhythms of meditation. However, during the Rebirthing Breathwork, we have also created a high-energy level with the connected breathing rhythm and perhaps it is this that enables access to the subconscious. Some specific connection with thoughts and wisdom from the depths of our psyche can take place and memories may begin to filter through, to appear in the waiting void. The increased mental sensitivity, created by the higher energy level in the brain, picks up these realisations and releases them to the conscious memory. When recalled and revealed during the integration of the breathing session, this phenomenon often helps us to understand and explain certain personal characteristics that are blocking our relationship with the self and others and tangling us in a struggle with life.

We have seen that the physical result of Rebirthing Breathwork practice is to increase the level of energy circulation in the body. The sensations associated with this increase can be temporary feelings of tingling in the skin of the hands and feet or around the mouth, can be shivering cold reactions or hot flushes, there can be moments of numbness felt in various parts of the body. Each one of these sensations has a particular explanation, as each individual is unique. The accompanying mental reaction that goes side by side with these physical experiences is also very interesting, as the holistic process seems to facilitate a release of memories stored in the subconscious zones of our minds.

Meaningful life
Rebirthing Breathwork involves a holistic approach. It serves not only to untangle chronic difficulties and struggles but also open up connection with joy, creativity and development of abilities. We can also choose to go into this process simply to involve ourselves in personal development, seeking to transform our behaviour with the motivation to live a joyful, lively, pleasant and more meaningful life.

One of the key elements of Rebirthing Breathwork is making the connection with this inner source of knowledge. The source of the learning is oneself. The realisations and information are released from within, giving you the opportunity to feel the power and the value of your own experience, adding value to what the Breathworker and therapist could be telling you about your amazing qualities, or the roots of your problems. The personal source makes the information much more difficult to deny than when the information is given to you by others. When you are breathing in a session, it is you who is in the driving seat, you who provides the motivation to continue or wind down and you who must find the courage to keep going when the process gets tough. This aspect increases our sense of self-worth and develops the confidence to believe in our inner wisdom and ourselves. Upon this base, we can then develop the strength of the foundations for our relationships with others.

Another attraction is that once you have learned the breathing technique through practice and experience, it becomes a valuable personal asset that you will take with you and use by yourself, wherever you go. You can practice short intervals of conscious connected breathing, unnoticed by people around you, at many different moments of your day, when you sense a need to calm yourself during a conflict, or before taking an important decision. Breathing can bring renewed clarity to a pathway or relationship where confusion exists or hesitation has appeared.

Relaxation and stress cannot exist at the same time in the same place, therefore the more we breathe consciously, the more time we will be relaxed and the less time we will be in stress. Easy equation.

Holistic therapy
There are different types of stress and the reference here is to stress produced by experiences that were neither accepted nor integrated into our life, with a subsequent development into traumas. These were probably situations generated by fear, shame, anger, loss, or other limiting emotions and were experienced at an age when we were unable to manage the event, or the perception of the event. The situation could have occurred in a moment of extreme vulnerability, creating a wound that couldn't heal completely. Searching to survive to the pain, we learned how to create a variety of defence mechanisms, but the wound remained there, getting deeper, becoming chronic and sometimes extremely acute.

Following through the therapeutical journey of understanding and healing the wounds of such experiences is a must for a return to balanced life. Holistic therapy is a choice that uses energy work such as Rebirthing Breathwork alongside with the psychotherapeutic process. We are holistic beings and we need to heal in all our dimensions (body, mind, emotion, spirit/meaning).

Such healing processes can include learning to express, to feel and to understand. releasing, resolving and transforming, leading us to accept and integrate, benefiting then from the joy and the bliss of the intimacy with yourself and your partner.

Each healed wound may leave a scar. Those scars are the testimony of the journey of healing and as such we can even be proud of them.

When those wounds were still open and unattended, an accumulation of difficult situations or some new and acute stress could lead us to a breakdown. However, once the wounds have been attended to and have healed, even though we are carrying the scars, when similar situations appear, we will be able to break through them and learn from the experience. This is what I call "Emotional Freedom".

Consciousness of abundance

Essentially, breathing and thinking are two personal inner resources that are available, simple, natural and powerful. Both open doors towards recognition of the state of our inner self. A third resource comes from the talents and the natural gifts that every person possesses; These are part of their own raw materials. Whether developed or not, these three resources will always be people's allies in times of crisis and in times of creativity.

Healing processes that have assimilated and developed the expression of these three inner elements, internally and externally, will always be valuable and successful. We live, breathe, relax and breathe, live, relax in a circular rhythm. Life has multiple points of connection in the midst of this rhythm that are connected to other directions of expansion. A person who keeps their intention and attention focused on their feelings, emotions, thoughts and memories, experimenting with and accepting these different phenomena will accept and heal their stress.

Acknowledging and accepting our divine origin and becoming co-creators of many things that we choose, will lead us to thoughts that are nourishing, thoughts that will lead us to actions that will help us to meet our needs.

The inner wisdom of the Self is that our potential is unlimited. By submerging ourselves in the satisfaction of creating and producing adequate results at the right moments of our lives, we become conscious of the nature of abundance. We can then develop the capacity to be relaxed, to accept and 'let go'. We will become an evolution of the Self that lives with emotions, thoughts and actions in a fresh and different perspective. This creates a new dynamic in life's process. From this consciousness, it becomes easier to transform stress, which is nothing else than the idea that we are short of time, resources and possibilities. Released from stress we can experience the magnificent feeling of living and loving fully in a world of sustainability where we are joyfully relating, creating, achieving, expanding, sharing and taking care of our surroundings.

Coming back to intimacy

How does breathing consciously help us to develop intimacy in our relationships? We have seen that conscious connected breathing is a valuable tool for knowing ourselves more completely and that our intimate relationship with others depends strongly on the nature of the intimate relationship we have with ourselves. The clarity with which I see myself is the fundamental groundwork of intimacy. It doesn't matter how long it takes me, the goal is to acknowledge and accept both my strengths and weaknesses, for only then will I be able to put aside 'pretending to be' and the 'wearing of camouflage' in the relationship and other misleading self-defence mechanisms.

This requirement applies as much to our physical sexuality as it does to the traits of our personality. Being confident and relaxed with our own bodies allows our partner to enjoy the same release. The more we manage to appear completely and truly as we are, the easier it will be for others to love us. Relationships are so much simpler when 'what you see is what you get'. This is the way we will attract people into our lives who are important to us.

Breathing and being well oxygenated helps us to be more present. Being more present helps us to deal with daily situations more easily. Dealing with situations in time and effectively, eliminates much stress. In the absence of stress there is relaxation, contemplation and awareness and from that state of being, the multitude of potential moments for enjoying short moments of intimacy with our beloved partner trends towards the limitless.

7 fundamental elements of Holistic Therapy and of life itself.

1-Breathe consciously, being aware of your thinking.
2-Inhale, recognizing who you are.
3-Exhale, letting go of what you no longer need.
4-Be present, asking clearly for what you want.
5-Accept and forgive, giving with love and generosity.
6-Keep on improving and expanding with gratitude.
7-Open your heart, letting in love and taking care of your surroundings

About this journey of life

Acknowledge an old song of truth
Accept each new experience
As a possibility for understanding
An opportunity for learning
Ride on the spiral
Searching out the illusions
Of the obstacles in your path

Inhale the precious life force
Witness the energy of desire
Dance and Dive into rhythms
Swim with streams
Recognise your good fortune
To be alive, aware and breathing
Conscious of the whirling cycles
Of this joyful journey of life

Who Makes the Bed?

Chapter Eleven
Image and Intimacy

Through our life's journey, we may change countries, move house, or change the friends we go out with. Aspects of our personality may get highlighted or diminished, our body shape may change, but the pigmentation of our skin and the colour of our eyes remain fundamentally the same, as do the core elements of our personality.

These are the essentials of whom and what we are and the secret of feeling and looking good is being in harmony with those essentials. So, it follows that certain blends of colours and styles of clothing will suit us beautifully and there are others that do not.

Strong base for success
Feeling confident, relaxed and comfortable with the image that you have of yourself is a strong base for success with intimacy, whereas negative self-consciousness, self-criticizing and eternally feeling 'not good enough' are destructive attitudes very effective at sabotaging and preventing intimacy.

Creating intimacy through development of image
With a stylist's analysis of your body architecture and their advice on your personal colour harmonies, you can look great and feel wonderful. Precise knowledge about the colours and styles that suit you whilst out shopping transform you into an excellent personal shopper as you only purchase items that compliment who you are. By ceasing to buy clothes that you will rarely wear, your wardrobe will become smaller but much more effective, therefore more

sustainable.

Some people struggle for years with their appearance, but when they become aware of the importance of body image and self-esteem, there are three major pathways that they usually take. Some will go into processes of personal development, focused on internal attitudes, on doing what they value most, what nourishes their self-esteem. Others will focus on the external aspects of image such as hair colour and wardrobe style as they chase the image that they always dreamed about. The third group will use a combination of both these directions, looking within, understanding themselves and their personality and releasing traumas, whilst simultaneously developing the harmony of their colour choices, the suitability of chosen styles and other external aspects of their image. This is when Holism occurs. When harmonious choices of style, colour and image highlight our natural qualities and faithfully represent our personality they powerfully nourish our self-esteem and facilitate the holistic presence of intimacy in our relationships.

We are creatures of body, emotion, mind, spirit and meaning. Attending to all these aspects of our existence is what creates our balance in life.

To wear or not to wear

We have touched deeply on the many inner aspects of the self in other chapters of this book and now is the time to approach the subject of our personal image; How to feel great and be comfortable independently of our gender, our age, the shape of our body and the natural physical changes that our bodies go through. How to feel confident and pleased about our look and the personal assets we already have. How to feel less concerned about what others think, while receiving more compliments than ever before for simply being yourself with the colours and style that suit you best. This is really a marvellous feeling, with gratitude for your efforts and the clarity and work of the consultant/stylist in colour and image who helped you to achieve this state.

A particular style and colour can look fantastic on the mannequin in the display window of a shop, but is not necessarily the right colour or style for your particular body. Studies show that women use a mere 15% of their wardrobe for 85 % of the time, meaning that their wardrobes contain much more than they need or that they have made many wasted purchases that they don't like.

This points to the unsustainable nature of much marketing, for when a person uses the wrong colour, they will tend to look older, faded and unfocused and will have to make more effort to show who they are.

What is colour

You have a unique skin tone and eye colour, which means some colours you choose to wear are in harmony with you and make you look great, and some have completely the opposite effect. By understanding what colour is, we can understand why we look good in some colours and not in others.

Colour is how we describe the visual effect of differing wavelengths or frequencies of transmitted light. Monochromatic light is light of one particular frequency. White light is the mixture of all the frequencies. A beautiful example of this is the wonderful rainbow produced by white sunlight shining on falling rain. As the white light passes through the water of the raindrops, it is refracted and separated into many different wavelengths, creating a whole rainbow of different colours.

When I see different colours, I am looking at different energy levels of light. When I see you and the colours of your face, I am seeing the light energy that is reflected from your face, your eyes and your hair.

The colour of the clothes you are wearing will also come to me as reflected energy of light, the 'right' colours of those clothes will be the colours which are in harmony with the natural pigmentation of your skin, the colour of your eyes and hair. A parallel situation exists in music, where notes whose frequencies are in harmony together create the symphony of pleasing sounds. Delightful clothes combinations have colours whose light frequencies are in harmony with each other and with the light frequencies of your natural skin tone and hue.

Feminine capital Image
Undertaking a transformational process of image change towards looking healthy and vibrant is easy when clothes and make-up are congruent and they enhance your look and become part of you.

Your choice of the right colour combinations in your wardrobe will get you feeling good about your look and looking well and healthy. By ensuring that your clothes flatter your body shape and allowing their style to display traits of your personality, you are creating an image that is personal and unique. Paradoxically, more attention will then be given to what you say and do rather than what you are wearing. You will be communicating efficiently as your most authentic self. Understanding the parameters, feeling and seeing the benefits of the correct colours, style and presentation of oneself brings about a major positive transformation in the way we perceive ourselves. This self-confident energy in turn works to transform how others perceive us.

In some leadership roles and in some countries, darker colours have been taken to be more authoritative. I know that many women dress in black and it seems that when they are in corporate business meetings, they feel that this permits all those present to blend together. Then it seems to me that they are all wearing the same uniform. We are also led to believe that black is slimming, so some women may think: 'I'll wear black again today, I could do with looking a few pounds lighter', but careful, the colour black does not suit everyone. For many, it is a very aging, lifeless colour; it can make you look invisible. You have to find which are your favourable dark colours, amongst for example say, navy, grey, brown, dark green, smoked grape, etc. In case of doubt, navy is often the safest. You can choose one of these and combine it with another colour and then with a detail of a third colour. This will give you enough contrast to ensure you stay memorable. Also, the accessories you choose can build impact. You will find your balance so you are looking just great, neither over-dressed nor underdressed for any occasion.

Remember this about black. If what you wear makes you invisible, then how you expect to be seen as confident, comfortable and secure as you want?

Two more important points, if you choose to dye your hair, it is crucial to know what hair colour base is the most suitable for your hue and similarly, when choosing the colour of the frames of your glasses.

Dare to use your feminine capital. Prepare yourself to stand out. You don't need to dress in the same uniform or in line with the men who surround you. In fact, disguising your femininity may even lead you to appear to be aloof, severe or unapproachable.

Initially, having a smaller wardrobe may create feelings of discomfort, but when all that you DO HAVE suits you well and is of harmonious colour and style, 'having less' becomes 'having more useable' and is often very liberating. Intelligent shopping and dressing then become fun and are not stressful. People will notice you for all the right reasons. Above all, you will notice yourself and like what you see, developing more and more confidence in yourself, thus building the foundation of the intimacy you could be looking for in your loving relationship.

Masculine capital image
As a man with a strong sense of self, you want to reach new heights of success independently of your area of expertise, you want to be heard, to be seen and to be respected.

Nowadays, men have many more choices of colour and style. Have fun with colours; it doesn't have to be loud, for some men for instance, it is about beautifully tuned harmony.

You know with shirts, it is all about the detail. The place to be very creative is with ties. As for suits, the most popular colour is dark. It will be important to check which of the dark colours is the best one for you, because although a black suit can look amazing on one man, it could look much less attractive on another and the similarly with brown. The safer ones will be the grey and the navy and even so, there are 'shades of grey' and navy. Focusing now on glasses, you may be wearing them all the time. So, it is important that they should be the right colour and shape for your face. A well-trained colour consultant will advise on the perfect choice for your uniqueness, helping you to enjoy your best impact, combining your set of colours.

It is also most important to respect your body shape and your character traits, to help you find your smart and comfortable style.

The same applies to your posture and the way that you hold your body. Independent of your age and weight, your masculine beauty can always be there. It is wonderful when a man is using his masculine capital to enhance his look and personality.

Embracing our best look
Our first impressions of someone are influenced by the way they are dressed and the image they display. Dressing enticingly has always been an art. Today, we have easier access to developing the ability to create a look of harmonious colours and style with tastefully chosen clothes and related accessories. It is a skill that everyone can learn

Using the right colours makes us feel positive and full of vitality just as wearing the wrong colours drains us and it can also alter our moods.

Remember, for some women and men, image is an essential

part of their personality, a part of their 'hygiene'. Therefore, image is as important for them as it is for others to be clean and orderly.

There are many people who would like to change some aspects of their lives, their personality characteristics or their image. This need has always existed and now expressing it is more acceptable. Successfully effecting changes has always been a matter of combining time, space and energy.

The more we embrace our true self and the colours that suit us best, the more we feel in connection with the self and others.

Terre d'Azile

Wind sweeping swiftly through leaf laden branches,
At times a whisper, then almost a whistle,
An appetising overture, harmonising vital colours,
Stretching open the wide horizons between two coasts.

Sapphire blue Pyrenean skies a boundless backdrop
To soft floating cycles of bright white cumulus clouds.
The golden sun star highlights a rainbow of petals.
Vivid reds, blushing pinks, burned orange, sunkissed yellow,
Bold purples flirting unashamed with deep organic greens
Among furrowed muddy brown hills of the rolling Arriege.

A visual symphonic beat dancing and reverberating,
The contained waves echoing back back again again,
Rebounding off jagged snowbound silhouettes.
Tangled angular crags, a boundary barricade to the South.

Familiar energy stirring within reaches deep into my spirit.
Homecoming to the warm love of welcome surroundings.
There where there's release from the daily freight of hurry,
I exhale a deep sigh, gently letting go into sweet peace.

Chapter Twelve
The Beauty of Touch

Relationship concerns the connection between people. It is about how we communicate with each other, how we relate with our family, our friends and colleagues and most importantly with our beloved partner or companion. it is a process of exchange and its success requires contact, connection and, above all, understanding.

Reach out a hand
In the context of the loving relationship, we depend largely on the spoken word to communicate our feelings and thoughts. We can also enjoy the pleasure of personal presence using the language of touch. For example, as we talk and listen, we sit close together touching knees, we exchange thoughts and gesticulate as we describe ideas, we hug away fears or kiss away tears, we tell stories and laugh together, embrace and dance with each other, reach out a hand to touch an arm or a cheek as we express wishes and maybe seek the support of a shoulder for our head as we confide our feelings.

Touch security and comfort
To understand how fundamental and primal this language is to us, imagine the foetus in the womb of the mother. As its consciousness develops and the senses begin to relay sensations to the growing awareness of the new spirit, the most constant sensations that are present, during those initial months of life, are the fluid warmth and the delicate enfolding contact of the containing uterus with the skin

of the foetus. As the unborn baby develops, those feelings of security and comfort are always associated with the experience of being contained, held and touched. It is no surprise then, to find that this strong and primal association between touch, security and comfort has such a lasting presence in our subconscious and conscious minds.

Our sense of touch

The skin is the largest organ of our body and has a number of important functions such as flexible and shock absorbing protection for the bones and the internal organs, temperature stabilisation both for cooling and warmth, discharge of toxins and natural self-repair of damage, to name a few. The sensitivity of the skin varies between the different zones of our bodies depending on their functions. For example, the surface of the heel will have a different sensitivity to the tips of the fingers. It is the surface of the skin that perceives touch and sends corresponding signals and sensations to the brain and there are a wide range of sensations that can be felt. Our sense of touch warns us of impending damage from extremes of heat, cold or pressure. It registers the pain of impact, cutting, tearing and piercing of the skin, but can also identify the contact of a gentle, secure and comforting loving touch as well as the sexually stimulating touches of love making.

Warm contact-rich bundles

Coming back to our example of the foetus, imagine now, the physical trials of either a natural birth with the unexpected sensations of severe, rhythmic squeezing or the liberating interruption of a delivery by Caesarean section and its implications, both of which are followed by noise, bright light and the shock of sensitive skin being cleaned and rubbed dry by towelling. After this experience, it is understandable that the new born finally finds comfort once s/he is gently and calmly enfolded in the mother's arms and feels again the soft warmth of skin-to-skin touch as the ritual of breast feeding begins. When we observe the way litters of kittens and puppies will naturally wriggle themselves together, tumbled into warm contact-rich bundles, we realise that we are not the only living beings on whom touch has such an important and nourishing effect. For the baby, touch sensations will continue to be a major source of information about the items that are present in the baby's life and, for a while, everything goes into the mouth for analysis and identification.

Recovering lost knowledge
In spite of this healthy beginning for the child and its strong contact with the benefits of touch, along the passage of the years through puberty into adolescence, the importance of touch for the growing youngster can diminish in favour of assertions of autonomy and independence. Furthermore, in the presence of 'role model' parents who are not at ease with open expressions of affection, love and tenderness, the adolescent's familiarity with touch, as a normal component of daily life, drifts gradually back into the depths of the memory.

Non-sexual touch
However, that is not the end of the story because, soon enough, the stirring flood of hormones propels the maturing adolescent into sexual awareness and a new encounter with touch, but now in its context as a sexual stimulation. This would all be in its place if it were not for the preceding loss of familiarity with touch, in its non-sexual capacity, to calm, to comfort and to heal. When we become aware of this process involving, for most young adults, the loss of the innocence of touch and its beneficial effects, we can understand why it could be of interest to recover our lost knowledge and our natural faculties concerning the language of sensitive touch.

Receiving and giving
A simple way to explore the domain of this language is to give yourself the gift of receiving a number of professional massages to help you relax and let go of stress and worries. Receiving good massage therapy generates feelings of being loved and valued simply for who you are. It contradicts the common belief that 'when I am being touched, it is only because something is expected from me in return.'

The pleasure of caring
To get more adventurous you could enrol in a school of massage and learn for yourself the power of human touch. You can learn how to soothe away stress and tension with your hands, dissolving headaches and back pains. You can develop your healing powers and encounter the pleasure of caring. This is something you can do as an individual and you can also participate together with your partner as a couple and bring into your relationship a new dimension of mutual loving care.

The Origins of Intimacy

*We stand facing our chosen pathway,
Your bright eyes lost in the depths of mine
Breathing deeply in rhythm and time,
Flushed, but willing to explore and discover,
Attracted by innocent impulse and healthy sexuality
To dive into this alluring energy of intimacy together,
Daring to take the simple risk of being truthful.*

*Myself in front of you, yourself in front of me,
Loving fiercely and unashamed, defences down.
Our body beauty, the work of natural magic,
Soft delightful curves, the promise of powerful contours,
Bathed in the warm fire light of our privacy,
But naked, armed only with our precious trust,
Self-confidence tangled and exposed, vulnerable
Amid the flow of confused contrasts of emotion.*

*Guiding me into learning, connecting me with love,
My first teacher, Mother of my nest of conception,
Taught me how to receive without conditions,
Fulfilled my needs with unbounded generosity.
I was also naked then and completely powerless,
But always nourished, warmed by her body heat,
Rocked and soothed in the fluid dimensions of her belly,
Blissed out in the comfort of the sensual caresses
Of the velvet, soft walls of my surrounds.
Intimacy has such unexpected origins.*

Who Makes the Bed?

Chapter Thirteen
Letting Love In

With today's media continuously emphasising how attractive and sexy looks should be, for some, the possibility of being loved seems directly connected to appearance. From such a conclusion, it is easy to get lost in obsessive behaviour focused on appearance only. Enticing clothing and a gym-tuned body shape are merely the start of the game. Plastic surgery can be undertaken to enhance our natural attributes, a tuck here, some silicone there, followed by Botox to rejuvenate the first tell-tale wrinkles and frequent visits to the hairdressers to colour away the inevitable appearance of those tell-tale white strands. Which are the actions that really develop self-esteem and which ones create more distance from self-love?

The enemy is us
Thanks to medical progress, we look forward to living for longer than before, but we do not easily accept that this may eventually mean looking older as we live those extra years. There is reluctance to mature gracefully into wisdom in our bodies and in our minds. We find it difficult to accept that we can be loved simply for who we are, rather than for who we appear to be. But the enemy is us, not the media, because the health of our loving sexual relationship depends much more on the energy that we bring with us into the couple than it does on our skill of conforming to the prevailing standards of sexiness and appearance.

The starburst of giving

The creation of joy, the making of love, can be an intimately shared activity where each of the lovers assume responsibility for their own pleasure and are able to ask clearly for what they need. By setting aside quality time to share intimate feelings and desires and informing each other about the loving gestures that bring the most pleasure, each partner of the couple can become familiar (practice makes perfect) with how to fulfil their partner's needs. Here they can experience the joyful starburst of giving and in return receive the pleasure of the sight and the sounds of the partner's spontaneous expressions of pleasure.

The yin-yang game

In Chinese philosophy, the concept of yin-yang can be described as the interaction of complementary rather than opposing energies or forces. We can think of active and passive or giving and receiving or demanding and accepting. The complementary forces interact to form a dynamic system in which the whole is greater than the parts. Relationships have both Yin and Yang aspects, to be a lover there must be a loved one in the same way that shadow cannot exist without light. Either of the two different energies may be seen to manifest themselves more strongly at different moments depending upon who the observer is.

Take time to play

So, let's have fun and do some relationship building. I can suggest a nourishing and fascinating game (good for all adults) that two can play, called Yin-Yang. To begin with, a rendezvous is made between the partners to meet up at a certain time and to be totally available for an agreed period (one or two hours?). Set aside an easy moment when the responsibilities and duties of the day have been accomplished. Mobile devices will be switched off and left outside the meeting place. A quiet room or space in the house, where no one may intrude, is jointly prepared in advance, with pleasant lighting and a warm floor covering.

What would you really like
The meeting begins with the couple, showered, relaxed and comfortably dressed, greeting each other in the space they have prepared. The choice is made as to who will be Yin and who will be Yang. To begin the game, the active Yang partner will lead and direct for the agreed time frame. Yang will think of what they would most like to receive from Yin and will ask for their wishes to be met by Yin, who does all he or she can to meet those requests. This does not involve Yin doing anything that they don't want to do. The aim is to give Yang the opportunity to think about their wishes and desires and voice them clearly, without worrying whether they are pleasing their partner or not.

Learning to receive
It is all about connecting with what you really want deep down inside. It is about being able to ask for what you want. It is about learning to receive without an obligation to give at the same time. It is also about being able to accept the refusal of a request. The game can be used to explore non-sexual desires as well as sensual and sexual experiences. You may ask to be massaged, to be told special things, or have your feet bathed in milk or to be cooked for. You may want to direct your partner in how you wish to be made love to.

Reversing the roles
The structure is very simple. For the agreed period of time, Yang determines the activities that they would like you both to do. You can ask for what you want and say how you would like it to be and during the experience, you can give feedback to your loving Yin about the way they are fulfilling your needs. When the agreed time

ends, feelings can be shared and thanks are given for the received generosity and, at the next session, the roles of Yin and Yang will be reversed, with the partner who first played the Yin energy taking their turn with the Yang.

Focus on giving
The role of Yin is to remain tuned in and receptive to the needs of their partner, focusing on giving and encouraging Yang to explore his or her desires and receive undivided attention. If Yin feels that Yang is asking for something that makes Yin uncomfortable, Yin just tells Yang 'I'm sorry, I can't fulfil that request just now, but I would be very happy to do something else. What else would you like me to do for you or with you?' and the game can continue.

Step into the open
This focus on the physical and spiritual pleasuring of the other is an important part of any couple's story. Perhaps we have never really, openly shared our fantasies with our partner; perhaps we have spent ages hoping that by some intuitive magic, they will understand what we need without us having to ask them. During the game, the camouflage of appearance is gradually set aside and we learn to step out in to the open. By revealing our deepest desires and wishes, we expose the sensitive and the secret. Revealing ourselves, we are preparing for true intimacy as we go beyond our conditioned limitations and shame. We are daring to appear as we are and experiencing the joy of being loved when we are in that vulnerable space. We begin to build a new understanding of ourselves and create a healthy self-esteem.

Transform the quality
The sources of pleasure during lovemaking can create intense and very beautiful physical sensations, however the pleasure can remain skin deep and the physical satisfaction, initially felt, can dissipate

itself quite quickly in heterosexual relationships. Some men can find it difficult to reach a really satisfying frequency of lovemaking with their partner, no matter how often they make love, they soon return to those needy feelings of dissatisfaction, as though the character of the lovemaking has become too routine and no longer quenches the thirst. Sometimes this can happen because the man has been focusing too much on his 'performance' and is not connected to sensing the energy that is there between the partners. His dissatisfaction can bring conflict and stress into the relationship as the woman finds herself being persuaded to have sex when she is not in the energy. Probably what is happening in these cases is that the level of consciousness being nourished by the sexual activity of the man is a rather physical one. How can we develop a different consciousness of what we are doing when making love? How can we transform the quality of the pleasure being shared to help it reach another depth of nourishment and satisfaction?

Breathe together love and play
In searching for something less fleeting, we may come across a deeper source of satisfaction. Bring in laughter, include fun in your sexuality, play with each other and set out to learn while loving and lovemaking. Dispose of the habitual expectations and requirements. Tear up the agenda. Practice breathing deeply and together during lovemaking. Breathe into the cyclic rhythm of the lovemaking, holding the visual connection between the eyes, then with eyes closed, try to visualise the flow of the energy between your two bodies between the streams of breath and the contact of the sexes. Extend the focus of your consciousness beyond the excitement of the physical feelings and make a connection with the energy being selflessly given to you by your partner during the lovemaking. This will require a relaxed and yet very focused presence. The space of intimacy is in there waiting to be discovered, a new tantric space where our hearts soften and open with gratitude as they fill with

pleasure and the awareness of receiving.

Connect with receiving

When you encounter this nourishing feeling, it is a rare moment and the feeling does not fade quickly. It is not a stimulation of the physical senses. It comes as a heart-warming flood of realisation of personal value that has been generated by the sensation of receiving love. The heart has opened to let love in. When experienced, this wonderful receptive connection with the other is a gift that will satisfy at a new and deeper level than the physical and take the mutual trust and intimacy existing between the couple onto a new plane. So, start today. Help yourself to grow beyond the shallow hungers of habitual sex. Breathe together, play with spontaneity, abandon disguise and concerns with image. Simply open your heart to love and let love in.

Life's gift

Life itself is a gift
Breathing in a conscious way
Exploring my realm beyond words.
Singing out a song of sounds.
With the voice of my soul
Dancing to the rhythm
With the music of my spirit.
Some actions I love immediately,
Others are complicated to accept.
Breathing, thinking and acting
In a conscious and connected way
I encounter the most precious gift of life,
The Acceptance of What Is.

Who Makes the Bed?

About the Author

Multi-award winner, Viola Edward was born in 1959 and her story highlights the turbulent experiences of a childhood fractured by her father's early death followed by migration and civil war. Further migration and cultural upheaval shortened her opportunity of growing up in a stable Lebanese family environment when as a teenager, together with her mother and sister, she was again relocated migration style, into the vibrant, colourful, yet unfamiliar South American culture of Venezuela.

Finding herself excluded from a traditional education, she set out on the pathway of alternative education that she remains on today. Through hard work and study in Caracas, she added Spanish and English to her knowledge of Arabic and French, completing high school and college through night classes.

Viola never let go of her dream of being a Psychotherapist. More so, she was a patient for several years in private and group sessions. Alongside her daytime work, Viola studied Transactional Analysis, Meditation, Rebirthing Breathwork Coaching and Transpersonal Psychotherapy.

In 1993, with eighteen years' experience of working in corporate environment, she renounced her career as successful marketing manager to follow her dream. She founded the 'Centro Rebirthing de Venezuela', a successful Holistic Breathwork Therapy Centre, specialising in Breathwork-Coaching Training, which she ran with her sister Layla. This was followed by the creation of 'Edward & Associates Business Consultancy'.

During this time Viola became increasingly involved in numerous

Holistic Business Consulting processes and Women's Rights issues, giving international lectures and seminars about Self-development, Addiction Prevention, Conscious Relationships, Breathwork-Coaching Training and Transpersonal Psychotherapy. Her book 'La Conciencia del Éxito y el Arte de Renacer' was published in 1999, translated to English as 'Breathing the Rhythm of Success' and also translated into Turkish as, 'Başarının Ritmini Solumak', in 2017 the Spanish tittle was changed to 'Respirando el Ritmo del Exito'

In 2003, at the age of 44, the whirling spiral of love brought her back to the Eastern Mediterranean where she married and set up a new home with her husband Michael de Glanville, in Cyprus. Together they established Kayana, a company focused on personal and organisational development. Obtaining a House of Colour franchise, she also became a Colour and Image consultant to enhance her colourful work throughout the Island.

Viola also hosts the program online "Feminine Capital Rhythm" and she collaborates with different international Magazines. Viola can coach in English, Spanish and Arabic

Now, at 58, she works with local and international clients at the Kayana Centre, located in Kyrenia on the north shore of the Island, looking down over the rustling olive trees to the sparkling, sapphire blue Mediterranean. She also travels abroad, lecturing and providing Breathwork training & sharing her experiences and her creations, one of the most well-known of which is the "Feminine Capital Rhythm".

You can find Viola at: www.violaedward.com

References

Allen, J. (1903). As a man thinketh. New York: Thomas Y. Crowell Company.

Bradshaw, J. (1992). Homecoming: Reclaiming and Championing Your Inner Child. New York: Bantam Books.

Chopra, D. (1992). The Seven Spiritual Laws of Success: A practical guide to the fulfillment of your dreams. Amber-Allen Publishing & New World Library.

Coelho, P. (1993). The Alchemist. New York: Harper Collins.

Griscom, C. (1990). The Healing of Emotion: Awakening the Fearless Self. Fireside.

King James Version. (n.d.). Book of Proverbs, chapter 23, verse 7.

Leonard Orr, K. G. (1998). Breaking the Death Habit: The Science of Everlasting Life. Berkeley: Frog Ltd.

Williamson, M. D. (1992). A Return to Love: Reflections on the Principles of "A Course in Miracles". New York: Harper Collins.

Bonus, From Her Next Book
Have We Met?

The Importance of Relational Capital in Sustainable Wealth

The Purpose
To go to the connection point that appears when women have embraced their femininity and men their masculinity, enabling the move into a sphere beyond the concepts of femininity and masculinity and where every individual is seen as unique with infinite possibilities, then togetherness is Sustainable.

Feminine Capital Rhythm: Breaking free from compromise
Encouraging the process of breaking free from compromises that women have made to fit into the masculine work world, this book is designed to help powerful achieving women in breaking free from restraints that prevent them from fully enjoying success and wealth. It seeks to identify and facilitate the development of personal feminine strengths and rebuild a no-compromise inner and outer attitude of pride and reliance on the energy of Feminine Capital.

Masculine Capital: Breaking free from cultural judgements
Dynamic support for the powerful men committed to breaking free of cultural judgements that prevents them from fully enjoying the company of women as peers in all areas of life.

Feminine Capital
A quick look at human history over the past years shows us clearly that following centuries of male domination, we have entered an era

of intense changes to existing social patterns.

One of the miracles of the twentieth century has been the intense feminine movement towards a harmonious balance of power with the masculine. Women have emerged as peers to men in the established order. They are now actively present in influential positions in Government, in Business, in Law, Science and Medicine and many other fields that were previously the reserves of the male.

However, along this pathway to equality, the powerful and successful woman has paid a huge price in her holistic health (body, mind, emotion, spirit, relations...) because she copied the established masculine model in order to unlock and enter his protected domain and be considered a peer. This has led her to damage much of her fundamental natural feminine energy.

So, there is a huge need for men and women to build equilibrium within themselves (of their own masculine and feminine energies) and between each other, whether this be in friendships, in loving relationships, in the workplace or in any other shared areas of life. It is my belief that key for this conflict resolution is for all to get in touch with their feminine energy.

To encourage such a process of transformation, I have developed the Feminine Capital Rhythm Program to bring awareness of the compromises that have been made, to identify and facilitate the development of personal feminine strengths and rebuild a no-compromise inner and outer attitude of pride and reliance on the energy of Feminine Capital.

The Feminine Capital Rhythm program is a strong, healing pulsation helping powerful women to break free into this uncharted territory, armed with the courage required to fully enjoy their success and good fortune without compromise. The program uses holistic self-knowledge, breathwork and image awareness.

So how does the notion of the rhythm of breath enter into this work? I believe that the rhythm of breathing has none of the same limitations as does a spoken language - it is a primal form of communication that envelops our entire body. It touches us profoundly, for it is sensed rather than seen, absorbed rather than heard. Like the heartbeat, some breathing rhythms are totally instinctive, while other rhythms are acquired during childhood because of their connection with emotions. We can develop and practice the strength and power of our chosen personal rhythms and we can learn to master them, understanding and feeling the ways in which their different pulsations affect our health and psyche, through the rhythm of the breath.

As a relationship psychotherapist, many people ask me how it is that we get it so wrong about our feminine and masculine energies. How have we managed to get into such energy wasting behaviours, considering the potential power of the diversity in feminine and masculine energies.

One of the answers is in the way we relate to others. Our outward appearance and our body language give out many clues to our identity and contribute towards the way we are perceived and how we are treated. There is a particular energy that appears in any interaction between two or more people, a Rhythm of connection. It is this energy that triggers our inner feelings of safety and trust, or discomfort and distrust, prompting the instinctive protective barriers to soften or to get harder.

Nowadays, we have so much knowledge about feminine and masculine energy. We also know about the extreme bright and dark sides of each of them. Some women damage themselves by following the most difficult of pathways, the shadow side of the masculine energy (rigidity, control, not expressing feelings, strictness, limitation and disconnection), while at the same time over compensating with their image to look more seductive.

Meanwhile the man, having lost a patriarchal kingdom that he has known for centuries, has needed to learn how to relocate himself in order to live the harmony of this new equation. This process also has been very difficult and frequently he will go into the shadow side of the feminine energy (being dependant, victimised, volatile, dispersed and manipulative). These are unfortunate scenarios for both genders and also the new generations growing up in their care.

By practicing the Feminine Capital Rhythm, women will feel how it is to be holding firm to a position or not. They can connect with the unquestionable strength of a NO or a YES and even the persuasive gentleness of a mutually benefitting arrangement. This energy rhythm is a woman's precious Capital. It is already there within her. Opening her awareness and diving into the knowledge, she can begin to see and appreciate it.

Like a healthy and solid capital transaction, Feminine Capital is built up by breaking free from the compromises that have kept women hooked into low self-esteem and low worth in certain area.

To create this Capital, she learns to live within the bright sides of both Feminine and Masculine energy. She frees her breathing from emotional and physical restraints. She embraces the holistic right to work, rest and be entertained, to love and be loved and to live the beauty of her motherhood. She continues to be creative, to change and age gracefully and to be a woman with pride in her heart.

She learns to be fully comfortable while being successful and wealthy, keeping the loving connection with all of her body and its beauty beyond her age. Always connected with her breathing force, life force. She can fly as high and as wide as she wants.

Testimonials

Hello everyone, I'm Sonia Pirona and my life is better now. When asked about Viola Edward; I have only kind words to say. I met her two decades ago, during times of hardship when I waywardly felt that I was the most unfortunate person in the world.

It was then, as often happens, that a single word opened the gates to possibility; Therapeutical Breathwork / Rebirthing. Wham! That was what I needed, I said to myself, to be reborn and fix the mess I thought was my life.

Then Viola arrived … The day I met her I loved her. Later, I loved her because it was so easy for me to feel her love; I then loved her for her discipline; I loved her more for her devotion to others without time or space; I continued to love her when, helpless, she gave me shelter amongst her people; a thousand times I loved her for the patience of her faith in me; I loved her even more for love itself, for that great strength that I am and that I desperately searched and searched for until Viola arrived.

Today, I love her. I must say that with her passion as her gift, she created the most prestigious and serious organisation of Therapy, Breathwork/Rebirthing in Venezuela, succeeding in developing this practice into an important movement within the therapeutic community of this country, both individually and collectively as well as encompassing business consultancy.

Yet she was able to not only create this fabulous movement in Venezuela, but trans-nationalised Breathwork/Rebirthing across several countries in South America, the Caribbean and Spain, where she bore the fruits of her passion as gifts.

Through her positive experience as a 'teacher' of Coaching and Rebirthing, she managed to organise the vast and intangible information on Conscious Connected Breathing and Energy. She was able not only to create a theoretical and practical manual based on the theories of Rebirthing, but she also enriched these with her own proposals on mission, vision and achievements, applicable to both individuals and business groups.

I was a member of the V Rebirthers' Training of Venezuela. There were about 15 people, both men and women. Whenever we meet, I feel a brotherhood of soul with them. Some of us used Breathwork as a platform and springboard for our subsequent searches, nowadays, in my case, with the absolute certainty that it accompanies me at all times.

I continue on my mission to speak and write so that others are able to find their own mission statements. Right now, I'm linking Biodanza and Automatic Writing as literary inspiration.

I am a poet, author and a chef. I work as a journalist in print media and online, for quite a while now I have been working with my Inner Master, with whom I reflect on life.

If I am speaking with you at this moment, it is thanks to, amongst millions of other stars, Viola Edward. My respects.

Sonia Pirona Salazar
Poet, Author, Journalist and Chef.

Viola was recommended to me by a friend in Cyprus. My friend had so much energy and such a positive outlook after working with Viola. I knew Viola would help me too.

Before I met Viola, I felt generally down. I was like a dog that had been left in a rehoming centre for too long: forlorn and a bit desperate!

I had a relationship problem and my behaviour was constrained by this and by unresolved issues from my past concerning my family.

I felt very guilty and was no longer able to feel happy.

Viola helped me to understand how past experiences affect my behaviour and how I react in certain situations. She allowed me to rise above these influences and I was able accept them and move on.

She is a supportive influence who gives practical strategies that have been helpful in dealing with feelings of disempowerment.

As a result of my time with her I feel happier, more free and I'm looking forward to the future.

Thank you.

And I'm a better tennis player, ha!

Thomas S.
Entrepreneur

I met Viola in mid-1997, when I was searching for help with my way of being. The first thing that struck me about her was her modesty in conveying her wisdom, doing so with simplicity and depth. I then discovered her commitment and her passion for truly connecting with people and her innate ability to 'accompany them' during their process, both inside and outside of the Rebirthing sessions (something which very few therapists do and which was instrumental at the start of my recovery).

I was privileged to be at her side when she ruminated aloud her ideas and annotations for her first book, and then to assist her in reviewing its editing, and later on to review the online publication. Privileged because I was learning more and more with her: about Rebirthing, about being the director of a holistic centre, about being a person. It was important for me to find the best way to bring written explanations on the subject to future readers, but conjugated in a way that remained as faithful as possible to her way of thinking and feeling.

So, by her side, her philosophy of life resonated with me and enveloped me; but after just a few months of reading and re-reading the paragraphs and chapters of that book, the importance and transcendence of consciously working with breathing and thinking (Rebirthing) conclusively permeated me. It was a blessing to accompany her during the 'birth' of her first book, back in 1999.

To her readers of any of her article and books: in order to understand this subject there is only one thing that would complete the reading, and doing the suggested exercises of her books, 'Breathing the Rhythm of Success' and 'Who makes the Bed', and that is to practice: take a Breathwork/Rebirthing course or any other course with Viola!

Over time, I have returned several times to her articles and her first book in order to rethink a personal or work matter through its vision. I will do the same with this her second book. So, just in case my gratitude was not enough…here it is again … Thank you!

Yolanda Farrais Valencia
Pedagogic Science, Breathworker/Rebirther, Lecturer.

Why People Should Have Holistic Psychotherapy?

I have met many people in my life, and I can honestly say I know very few who, in my opinion, are totally well balanced and 100 percent content. From a friend who nursed her mother until she died in her 50s from cancer, another friend who suffered from an eating disorder to the numerous people I know who have lived with feuds between their relatives that ripped the family apart, or those who have grown up with divorced parents and those who are struggling with their sexuality, or can't seem to hold down a relationship, we all have some 'stuff' going on in our heads that would benefit from a mental spring clean. An emotional work out if you like. Having struggled with depression and some addictive tendencies for many years I decided to embark on psychotherapy in a bid to stop myself sinking lower into the mire.

I have been seeing my psychotherapist, Viola, for a couple of months now and I believe it is something that many people would benefit from.

A lot of people, myself included, believe that psychotherapy is a very self-indulgent notion. A luxury of the rich and privileged west. It is unlikely that families living in poverty, wondering where their next meal will come from or how to keep a roof over the heads would concern themselves with trying to sort out their feelings of depression or low self-esteem, for example. These days there are psychotherapy, psychiatry, psychoanalysis, psychology and it can all be a little confusing to differentiate between these different disciplines. While connected, they are all different. Psyche comes from the Greek for soul so to a degree they are all about trying to fix the soul to help people lead a happier life.

I certainly have very little knowledge and I don't want to get technical. Popular internet site Wikipedia (though not infallible it can be an interesting source of research) says: 'Psychotherapy is a general term referring to therapeutic interaction or treatment contracted between a trained professional and a client, patient, family, couple, or group.' Through psychotherapy, psychotherapists attempt to help people live happier, healthier and more productive lives. Those who visit psychotherapists can be suffering from any number of problems from addiction to long term ill health and low self-esteem to relationship problems.

Let me tell you a little about my journey. I had a very mixed childhood, some blissful memories and some really dark ones. I was an expert at pushing my feelings and emotions, my reactions to the stuff that happened in my life, deep inside me. To a place where I didn't have to deal with it. I left school with decent grades but at college I started to smoke cannabis, heavily. I failed my A-Levels, I didn't go to university and the heavy smoking continued for the next 17 years. The heavy drinking started about 5 years-ago and an unpleasant experience which occurred during the year I became 30 compounded my problems and became an excuse to drink and smoke more. Don't get me wrong, there have been some fantastic times in my life and I am lucky enough to have an incredibly supportive family and some great friends.

However, this doesn't change the fact that the smoking and drinking continued and the use became heavier. I would drink before I went to work, when I finished work, on my days off. Any chance. And we can all make the chances or think of an excuse. The depression got worse and I felt lower and lower. The time had come to try and deal with my demons. I remember telling a member of my family that I wanted help to 'untangle what feels like a big ball of wool in my head'.

Meeting Viola has had a big impact on me. It has helped me understand the things that have happened in my life. To see more clearly why those close to me have made the decisions they have and taken the actions they have. The anger is not as strong as it was but instead is being replaced with some sort of compassion and forgiveness. There is still a way to go and the depression hasn't disappeared but I am on the right path.

Who Makes the Bed?

Before I left London and came to Cyprus I stopped buying cannabis and smoking it. It wasn't easy as I had been doing it for so long and it had become habitual. But I did it and it has now been more than two months since I have smoked any. The drinking is the addiction I am struggling with but with Viola's help I am combatting it.

I guess what I am trying to say is that we spend our time going to the gym and maintaining our physical health. We do crosswords and Sudoku puzzles to increase our brain power. We eat fresh fruit and vegetables and watch our diet to stave off illness and maintain a sense of physical good health but what about our emotional wellbeing. How about a work out for your soul, your psyche, your emotions? I believe it is as necessary as any other form of 'exercise' we indulge in and can only bring positive benefits.

Olivia D.
Journalist

Hey Viola, I hope all is well, I would just like to apologize for not thanking you properly and on time for giving me an open-minded infrastructure. I have a great relationship with my dad now, he is more like an older brother to me and I am in the 2nd best school in Cyprus about to finish my diploma and certificate then heading off to some more training in my favourite sport, then a gap year travelling, then to college. I really feel that if it wasn't for you I would be on the spiral down in a rebellious fashion. So once again thank you so much and I hope you have success in your future life as you do now.

Take care and kind regards to Michael too

John P.
Teenager, Student

Working therapeutically with Viola is an experience of love. She is present, loving, giving, sharing, expressing, experiencing with you at all times. she is holding you up until you get your strength back to stand on your own. She is learning with you throughout your own journey and being open to all the new experiences and knowledge even after so many years of experience. And we love her for that, for her love, strength, caring, sharing, openness and support.

Nadir Aydin
Journalist, Interior Design and Entrepreneur

Viola Edward has helped me through her Coaching techniques to unleash my potential both in my personal and business relationships. Her emphasis on communication and free flow of expression is vital for any individual or institution.

Emre Osmanlar
Artist, Designer and Entrepreneur

My journey started 10 years-ago with this woman who makes me happy with my existence and with this philosophy I have taken the path of joy and success

   I was on my own and now I am married and mother of two beautiful souls.

   She is always next to me and her all clients, I don't know how she can do this successfully being professional and having her own family at the same time, she is a gift to us and to everyone thank you for being.

Hatice Ozalp.
Pharmacist & Organic Entrepreneur

I feel very privileged to have worked with Viola both as a client and as a collaborator; it has been very insightful and fulfilling. One can tell straight away that she not only has over 20 years' experience in the fields of Breathwork and Psychotherapy but that she is also naturally gifted in what she does. Viola is very present and aware of her clients' needs even if in large group rebirthing sessions.

Peter Petrou
Entrepreneur, Yoga Teacher

Viola encourages me to connect with other women in order to celebrate our uniqueness and spread firmly our alluring feminine energy.

Cenev Tatar
Artist and Illustrator